GUIDE TO

Succu

of Southern Africa

Gideon F. Smith

& Neil R. Crouch

FRONT COVER: *Huernia zebrina*
BACK COVER: *Gasteria batesiana* (top); *Opuntia ficus-indica* (bottom left) ; *Kalanchoe neglecta* (bottom right)
SPINE: *Aloe ciliaris*
TITLE PAGE: *Euphorbia enopla* var. *enopla*
ABOVE: *Euphorbia tetragona*
OPPOSITE: *Crassula coccinea*

Published by Struik Nature
(an imprint of Penguin Random House (Pty) Ltd)
Company Reg. No. 1953/000441/07
The Estuaries No 4, Oxbow Crescent,
Century Avenue, Century City, 7441
PO Box 1144, Cape Town, 8000 South Africa

Visit us at **www.randomstruik.co.za**

First published 2009
10 9 8 7 6 5 4

Publishing manager: Pippa Parker
Managing editor: Helen de Villiers
Design director: Janice Evans
Editor: Emily Bowles
Cartographer: Martin Endemann
Illustrator: Tanza Crouch
Proofreader: Tessa Kennedy

Reproduction by Hirt & Carter Cape (Pty) Ltd
Printed by RR Donnelley Asia Printing Solutions Ltd

ISBN 978 1 77007 662 4 (PRINT)
ISBN 978 1 92054 418 8 (EPUB)
ISBN 978 1 92054 419 5 (PDF)

Acknowledgements

Hannelie Snyman of the National Herbarium of the South African National Biodiversity Institute in Pretoria kindly assisted with accessing PRECIS data, used in part to compile some distribution maps. For access to properties on which photographs were taken the following landowners or facilitators are gratefully acknowledged: Suseth and Sterling Pienaar of the farm Aasvoëlkrantz near Nieu Bethesda; Christopher Dalzell, Curator of the Durban Botanic Gardens; James van Vuuren of Ulundi; Jens Juterboch and Susan Clark of Cullinan; John and Sandie Burrows of Buffelskloof Nature Reserve; Doug McMurtry and Shane Burns of Whytethorne. David Styles, Ben Pretorius and Ben Botha, all of Durban, kindly allowed photography of their living collections. Priscilla Burgoyne of the National Herbarium helpfully commented on various odd images and plant material. Financial assistance from the University of KwaZulu-Natal in support of fieldwork is gratefully acknowledged. Jay Govender of the School of Chemistry has kindly and efficiently administered these financial aspects. The team at Struik Nature has professionally and efficiently taken this project forward; we are especially grateful for the support of Pippa Parker, Janice Evans and Emily Bowles in this regard. Lastly, thanks to Tanza Crouch for the illustration on succulent life forms (p. 5), and her great company while out in the field exploring the amazing world of succulents.

CONTENTS

INTRODUCTION

Much of southern Africa is semi-arid to arid, indeed desert-like, and it is perhaps not surprising that succulents abound in the region. Somewhat predictably, therefore, southern Africa can also lay claim to having the richest and most diverse succulent flora in the world. Although this has been known for many years, the extent and diversity of this was only recently verified by a comprehensive survey of this group. The results revealed that an amazing 47 per cent of the world's known succulents occur in southern Africa.

Angora goats grazing selectively in the *noorsveld* near Jansenville. The landscape is dominated by *Euphorbia caerulescens.*

Succulents come in all shapes and sizes. This diversity ranges from succulent forest, savanna and desert trees of over 20 m tall, such as the baobab, to miniature soil-huggers only a few millimetres high that mimic their pebble-desert surroundings. One thing they all have in common is the ability to store water in one or more of their organs for later slow release. Whereas plants in moist regions absorb water and immediately release it through their leaves, succulents have developed a range of mechanisms allowing them to accumulate moisture when it is available, and thereby sustain plant growth when they are water-deprived.

What are succulents?

Succulents are plants that store water in one, or all, of three organs – their roots, stems or leaves – to enable them to survive droughts. In some species, the continuum between the roots and stem becomes swollen and expanded to form a so-called caudex. When these 'caudiciform' succulents are cultivated with their fat 'feet' exposed, the plants make spectacular specimens. However, two mainstays of succulents in general are the leaf and stem succulents. Other types less commonly encountered – succulent inflorescences and above-ground bulbs – are shown on page 5.

Examples of the main types of succulent life forms

A Leaf succulent (*Kalanchoe thyrsiflora*); **B** Stem succulent (*Euphorbia avasmontana*); **C** Inflorescence (*Bowiea volubilis*); **D** Pachycaul (*Adenia fruticosa*); **E** Epigeal bulbs (*Albuca* sp. nov.); **F** Caudiciform (*Gerrardanthus macrorhizus*).

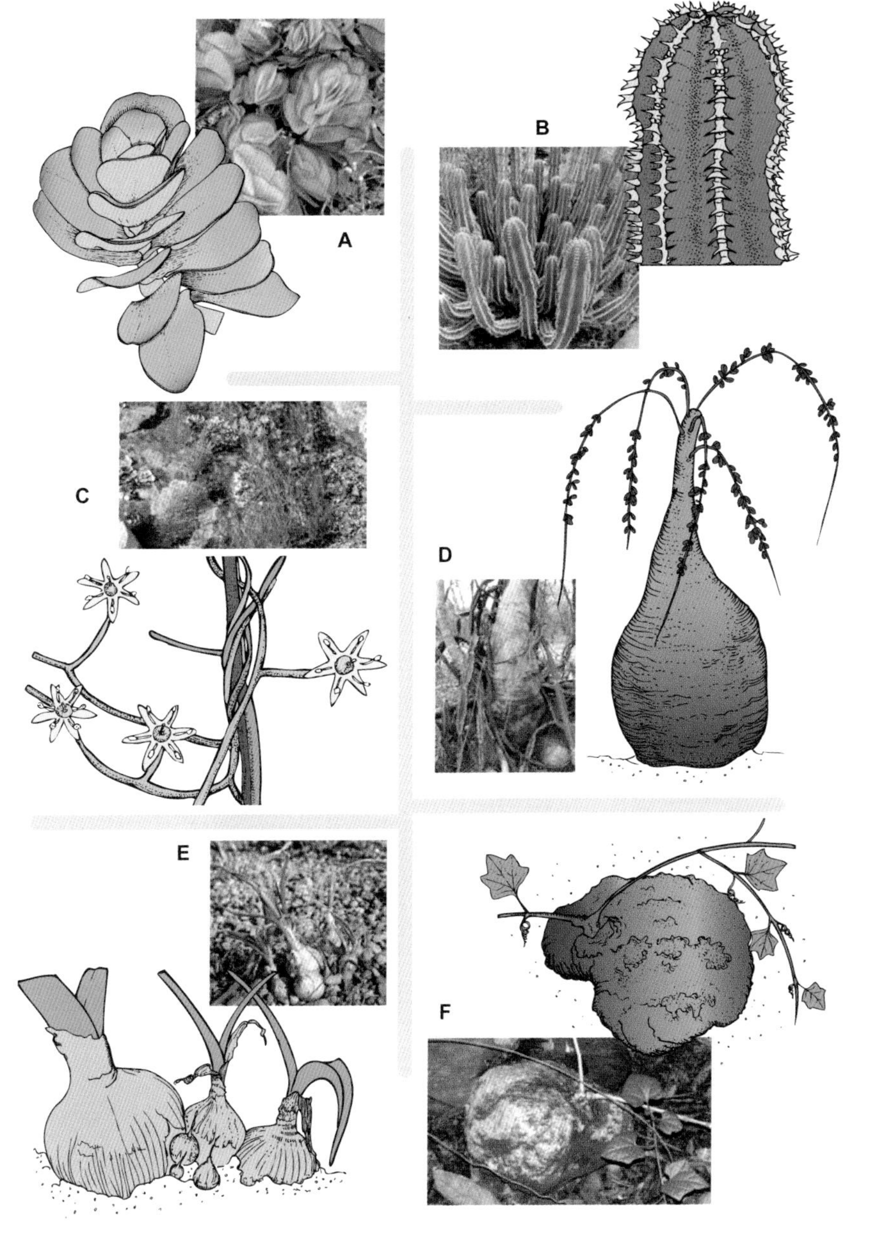

Succulents have attracted considerable attention over the past centuries for, among other things, their often bizarre forms. And with nearly half of the world's succulents occurring in southern Africa, the region is the primary hotspot for this life form.

Conservation alert!

Some succulent species are increasingly in danger of having to give up their habitats to development, or other pressures, especially where they occur close to ever-expanding large cities. *Aloe bowiea*, endemic to the Coega area near Port Elizabeth in the Eastern Cape, is one of these and arguably the most threatened of all South African aloe species.

The resemblance of *Lithops lesliei* plants to female genitalia has suggested their traditional application in love charms and potions for a variety of gynaecological problems.

Many of the smaller succulent plant species mimic their surroundings. The angular leaves of *Stomatium mustellinum*, from near Bethulie in the southern Free State, closely resemble the shape and drab brown colour of the surrounding pebbles.

The rocky hillsides around Springbok provide an ideal habitat for a wide variety of *vygies*, crassulas and other succulents.

DISTRIBUTION OF SUCCULENTS IN SOUTHERN AFRICA

Succulent plants are distributed over the whole of southern Africa from the highest mountain top to the southernmost tip of the subcontinent, and from the arid west to subtropical forests in the east. The succulent plants from the warm-temperate western regions are mainly leaf succulents, whereas stem succulents are more common in the warmer, subtropical eastern parts of South Africa. The greatest concentration of succulent plants is found in the warm-temperate, semi-arid, winter-rainfall region known as the Succulent Karoo. Within this region, the Richtersveld, Namaqualand, Knersvlakte,

Distribution of succulent genera in South Africa, Lesotho and Swaziland

Note that distribution information is sometimes less comprehensive for countries north of South Africa, given the limited availability of herbarium records.

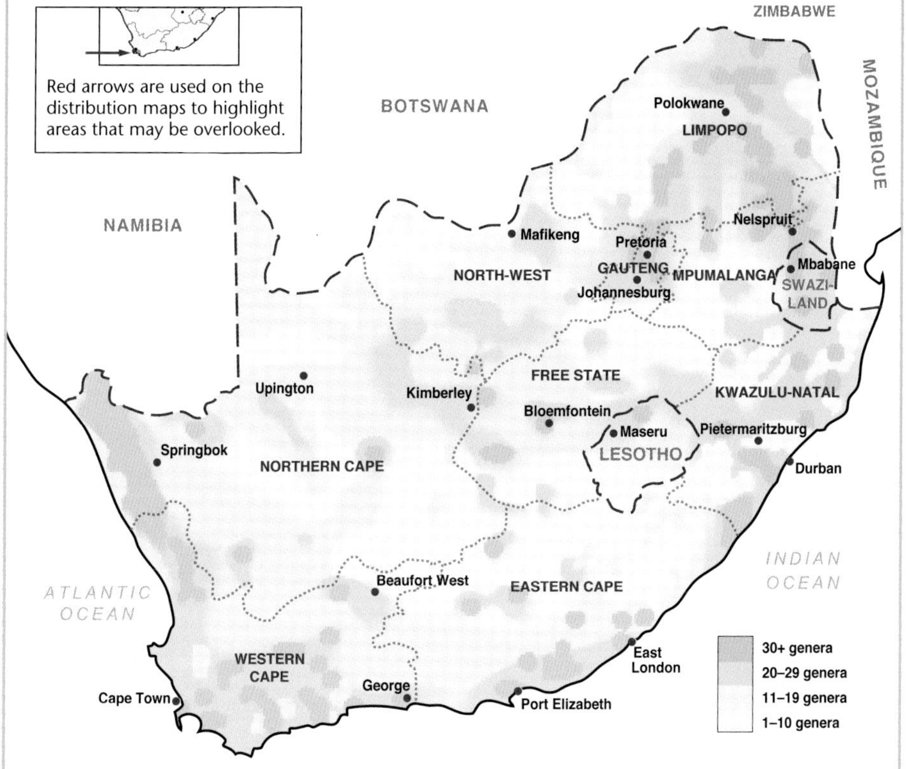

Red arrows are used on the distribution maps to highlight areas that may be overlooked.

ZIMBABWE
BOTSWANA
MOZAMBIQUE
NAMIBIA
Polokwane
LIMPOPO
Nelspruit
Mafikeng
Pretoria
NORTH-WEST
GAUTENG
MPUMALANGA
Mbabane
SWAZI-LAND
Johannesburg
FREE STATE
Upington
Kimberley
KWAZULU-NATAL
Bloemfontein
Maseru
Pietermaritzburg
Springbok
LESOTHO
NORTHERN CAPE
Durban
INDIAN OCEAN
ATLANTIC OCEAN
Beaufort West
EASTERN CAPE
East London
WESTERN CAPE
George
Cape Town
Port Elizabeth
30+ genera
20–29 genera
11–19 genera
1–10 genera

Worcester-Robertson Karoo and the Little Karoo harbour particularly high numbers of succulents. Over 1 000 species of the Mesembryanthemaceae (also known as mesembs, midday flowers or *vygies*) occur in this area. The southwestern Cape *fynbos* vegetation and the impenetrable thickets of the Eastern Cape are also surprisingly rich in succulent plant species, as are the Great and Upper Karoos, as well as the Bushmanland region, which all receive rainfall mainly in summer. Other regions noteworthy for their succulent plant riches include the northern and eastern subtropical summer-rainfall regions of southern Africa, the arid bushveld of river valleys in Mpumalanga, the thornveld of KwaZulu-Natal and the thickets of the eastern seaboard. Among the succulent plant families well represented in these regions are the Asphodelaceae (the aloes and their relatives), Apocynaceae (carrion flowers), Passifloraceae

View from the Valley of Desolation across the plains of Camdeboo, with *Aloe striatula* flowering in the foreground.

(passion flowers) and Lamiaceae (mints). Grasslands, too, have a high diversity of succulent plants, especially caudiciforms – succulents with large or small foot-like basal swellings – and some of the smaller crassulas and stapeliads, and even a few *vygies*. In contrast, the subtropical and warm-temperate forest regions have comparatively lower numbers of succulents, exceptions being the leaf succulent species of Crassulaceae and Piperaceae.

A number of succulents from other parts of the world have become naturalised in southern Africa, following their introduction by humans. Many of these plants are highly invasive and should not be cultivated. The maps accompanying the species accounts reflect present-day distribution data, but are bound to change as alien plants tend to colonise suitable habitats vigorously. In the text, alien species are marked with the symbol Ⓐ.

Aloe ferox in full winter bloom. This species has long been the main source of bitter aloe, known commercially as Cape aloes or aloe lump, an internationally important laxative medicine.

Paardekloof in the Eastern Cape is home to a wide range of Crassulaceae and Asteraceae succulent species, which grow among *Euphorbia tetragona* trees in the kloof and along the rocky hillsides.

Useful succulents

A child drinking the nectar of *Aloe marlothii*.

The relationship between succulents and humans in southern Africa reveals a fascinating cultural heritage. Plants that must survive periods of extreme stress, whether from cold, heat or drought, tend to be rich in secondary metabolites – chemicals produced by the plant that often provide medicinal applications. The multitude of different chemical compounds contained in the juices of succulents have for centuries attracted the attention of southern African user-groups, from the Nama in the west to the Xhosa and Zulu in the east. Examples include the *vygie Sceletium tortuosum* (*kougoed*) and *Aloe ferox* (the karoo or bitter aloe), both of which are known to possess bioactive compounds. Although a pharmacological rationale underpins the selection of many such plants, others appear to be 'Doctrine of Signature' subjects. In such instances the resemblance of plants to human organs or a particular ailment is believed to indicate their medicinal usefulness. In southern Africa a benign deity, 'Nkulunkulu', reputedly promotes these signs. For example, the milky sap of *Euphorbia woodii* is applied to the breasts of mothers to stimulate lactation. In similar vein, preparations from the cryptic forest species *Gasteria croucheri* are reputed to render Zulu warriors partly invisible during combat. Succulent species also feature strongly as protective charm plants, with the likes of kalanchoes, haworthias and crassulas grown close to homesteads to protect them from natural or orchestrated disasters such as lightning strikes and bewitchment.

Succulents serve many other uses, from sources of food (e.g. *Fockea edulis*, kambroo) and ropes (e.g. *Sansevieria aethiopica*, mother-in-law's tongue) to fibres for weaving (e.g. *Adansonia digitata*, baobab). To this day numerous succulents are offered for sale in traditional chemist stores or on street corners as part of the so-called *muthi* trade in southern Africa. In recent years, the importance of safeguarding biodiversity has gained prominence in discussions among concerned conservationists and politicians. These discussions range from how to ensure the sustainable supply of plant material for traditional magico-medicinal practices, to the large-scale agricultural production of sufficient food to feed the ever-increasing population of the subcontinent. In this debate succulents are playing an increasingly important role.

GARDENING WITH SUCCULENTS

Gardeners are becoming aware of the importance and wisdom of ecologically sound and waterwise gardening. With this in mind, increasing numbers of succulents are being made available in the horticultural trade, making it easier to plant and maintain dry, problematic areas in a garden.

Succulents remain radiant even – especially – during times of drought. They love both coastal and inland heat and can persevere through continental droughts and sea gales. These fat-bodied plants look good at most times, with their often greyish-white, wax-covered foliage that shimmers handsomely in the heat.

Succulents are long-lived and come in diverse shapes and sizes – there are species to suit every space. Some, especially creepers, will flop gratefully, if ungraciously, onto surrounding plants. Others take the form of majestic trees with large leafy canopies, while still others resemble the tiny pebbles among which they grow. They can also provide a blaze of colour at various times of the year (e.g. red crassula, *Crassula coccinea,* flowers in high summer and krantz aloe, *Aloe arborescens,* in the depths of winter).

In addition to their aesthetic appeal, some gardeners may cultivate succulents for their juice-filled leaves, roots and trunks, which have served as antiseptics and natural medicines since time immemorial. Whatever the reasons for their growing popularity, succulents are among the most useful and strikingly beautiful plants of the southern African landscape.

Aloe dichotoma, a slow-growing but rewarding subject for drier regions, seen here growing in a large pot in the Karoo town of Graaff-Reinet.

The thin-stemmed species of *Delosperma,* such as *D. scabripes,* are useful and attractive cascading subjects that break the monotony and harshness of block retaining embankments without completely obscuring them.

Magnificent *Aloe thraskii* specimens will enhance many an east coast garden setting.

Southern African succulents in world horticulture

Southern Africa has presented the world with a considerable number of succulents that are now globally popular in domestic and amenity gardening. These include species of *Pelargonium* such as *Pelargonium peltatum* (the ivy-leaved geraniums of horticulture), *Senecio tamoides* (canary creeper), *Carpobrotus edulis* (creeping fig), *Cotyledon orbiculata* (pig's ears) and *Aloe arborescens* (krantz aloe), to name but a few.

Large containers filled with a well-drained medium can present a wide range of colourful succulent subjects. This pot has been placed on the warmer northwestern aspect of a home to receive maximum afternoon sunlight.

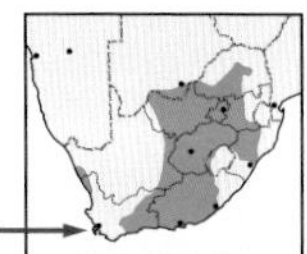

Agave americana var. *americana* Ⓐ

Century plant | *Blougaringboom*

Plants grow as massive, trunkless rosettes that sprout small plants extensively from the base. The blue leaves are very long and tend to flop to one side. They have marginal spines with a hard, sharp tip. After several years – sometimes as many as 25 – plants produce a single flowering pole that can reach up to 8 m skywards. These inflorescences carry numerous horizontal side branches that gradually become shorter towards the top, giving the pole a cone-shaped appearance. Flowers are yellowish-green and emit a strong, fruity odour, especially at night, indicating that they attract fruit bats. Originating in Mexico and the southern United States, it is widely naturalised in South Africa, but tends not to become a weed.

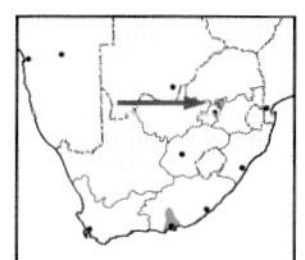

Agave angustifolia Ⓐ

Kleingaringboom

Plants grow as small to medium-sized rosettes that produce numerous off-sets at ground level to form large, impenetrable clumps. Leaves are fairly flat and sword-shaped. Leaf margins are armed with short, very sharp teeth, while the leaf tips carry a prominent, hard, dark brown spine. Inflorescences are produced after many years and resemble Christmas trees in outline. Greenish-yellow flowers are borne erectly on the side branches. Plants are invasive and should not be cultivated.

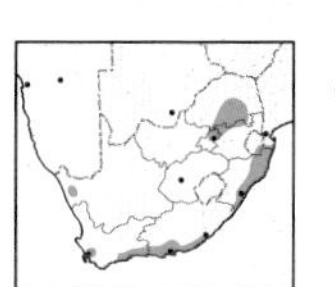

Agave sisalana Ⓐ

Sisal | *Garingboom, Sisal*

These large, trunkless rosettes sprout small plants extensively from the base. The dark green leaves usually lack marginal spines, but are very sharp-tipped. They always remain firmly erect, even after several years of growth. After some years – often fewer than 10 – plants produce a single, massive flowering pole that reaches up to 6 m. These inflorescences carry numerous widely spaced, horizontal side branches that give them a dainty, inverted cone-shaped appearance. Small, perfectly formed plants are carried on the inflorescence. Flowers are green and not as strongly scented as those of *A. americana*. The species, originating in Mexico, is widely naturalised in South Africa and has a tendency to become a weed.

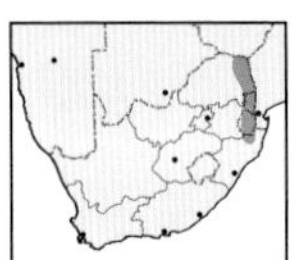

Adenium multiflorum

Impala lily, Sabi star | *Impalalelie*

Among the most attractive southern African succulents, these shrubs usually stand about chest high. The silvery succulent stems are leafless at the time of flowering (in late winter) and present an open architecture that gives the plants a bonsai-like appearance. The leaves are simple and clustered at the branch ends. Plants are easily recognised by the star-shaped, white flowers with their bright, reddish-pink petal margins. Bright red stripes are present in the throat of the broad floral tube. The species is found in dry lowveld vegetation.

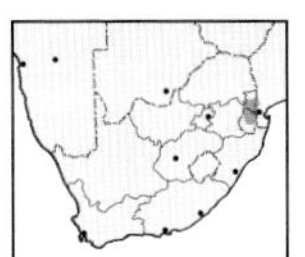

Adenium swazicum

Summer impala lily

These succulent shrubs only reach to about waist height in their natural habitat. Stems are swollen, and have a smooth, greyish-white bark. The uniformly pink blooms are produced from mid- to late summer while the leaves are present on the plants. The fruit consists of a pair of horn-like pods that release a mass of small seeds, each of which is crowned with a tuft of hairs to assist in its dispersal by wind. This species is restricted to the bushveld.

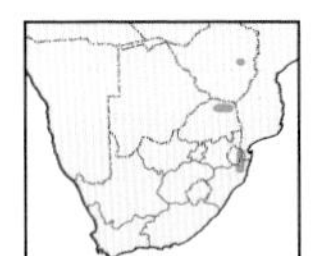

Australluma ubomboensis

Ubombo thick-boat

Though sometimes mat-forming, this dwarf stem succulent usually occurs as a small clump of stems, occupying a shallow soil pocket, or a crevice on a rock dome. It is also known to occur between rocks in dry, open woodland. The grey-brown to grey-green stems are well camouflaged, up to 8 cm tall and usually erect, although they are often found leaning over. They are four-angled. During summer, small purple-brown, star-shaped flowers are produced from the stem tips. Horned pods develop following successful pollination. Found in the drier regions of the eastern interior, mainly in the Lebombo Mountains.

Brachystelma barberae

Barber's brachystelma | *Platvoetaasblom*

The irregularly shaped tubers of this species, which often reach 15 cm in breadth, are frequently half exposed in their rocky, grassland setting. They bear a short, upright deciduous stem presenting egg-shaped, lightly hairy leaves. The inflorescence comprises a ball of cage-like flowers, each being about 4 cm long with five narrow, greenish lobes united at the tip. Inside, the flowers are dull purple and densely set with hairs that help to disseminate an unpleasant scent for attracting their carrion fly pollinators. An early flowering species that may be encountered blooming from August through to mid-summer.

Brachystelma bruceae

The prostrate stems of this dainty *Brachystelma* radiate from a medium-sized tuber growing in sandy quartzite-derived soils. Paired leaves adorn these shoots and have a slightly metallic appearance. The small, solitary, star-shaped flowers are produced towards the shoot ends; each bloom is a rich purple-maroon, shiny and without hairs. This species is found mainly in the vicinity of Kaapsehoop in Mpumalanga, where it flowers during the summer months.

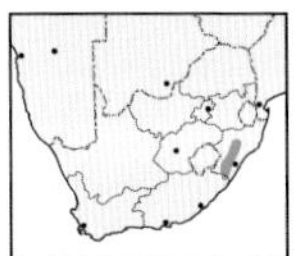

Brachystelma modestum

Named for its modest size, this species has a small tuber, sometimes exposed, from which a few upright to leaning stems are produced each year. These shoots bear little, paired leaves and the occasional star-shaped flower. Each bloom has five purple-tipped lobes and a broadly bell-shaped throat that is light yellow in colour. This is strongly marked with a series of near-concentric, narrow purple bands that lead to a purple base. It is found growing in shallow soil pockets on the edges of krantzes.

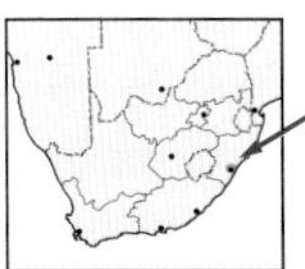

Brachystelma natalense

Plants grow knee-high from a claw-shaped, succulent underground tuber. The leaves are remarkably soft and densely covered in hairs, a characteristic that helps to distinguish it when not flowering from the very similar looking, but coarse-leaved, *Thunbergia atriplicifolia* with which it grows. The small, lime-green flowers nod at the end of thin, flowering stems during the summer months. Each flower is only a few millimetres across, and is star-shaped with five spreading lobes. During winter, the aerial plant parts die back to the stem tuber. A rare species, to date known only from the greater Durban surrounds, found growing in rocky grassland overlying Natal Group Sandstone.

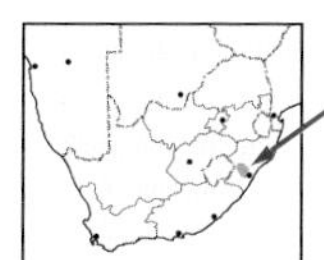

Brachystelma pulchellum

Beautiful brachystelma

This tiny *Brachystelma* hides for the most part under tufts of grass. From the small, slightly flattened tuber several thin, branched purple stems are produced, each lying flat on the soil surface and bearing pairs of little purplish-green leaves. These leaves become progressively smaller towards the branch ends. During summer, single, tiny, starfish-like flowers are produced from the nodes out of which the leaves grow. The youngest flowers develop towards the shoot tips. Each flower is maroon with creamy yellow banding in its mid-zone. Between each of the five dark lobes, the maroon tips of the calyx lobes are just evident. Found in shallow soil pockets overlying sandstone at the edge of krantzes.

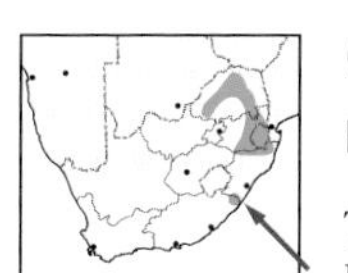

Ceropegia distincta subsp. *haygarthii*

Haygarth's ceropegia

The smooth, succulent stems of this low-growing creeper twine to a length of 2 m. One or two heart-shaped, fleshy leaves are present at each node along the stem. From spring to mid-summer blooms are produced on small inflorescences along the shoot length as it develops. The flowers are up to 5 cm long. The floral tube is globe-shaped at its base, thereafter bending upwards at a near right angle to present its expanded mouth vertically. At the flower tip the five lobes contract into an erect, wire-like tube at the end of which is a knob-like, five-winged structure. The length of this projection and the size of the apical knob are highly variable. The outer corolla is cream flecked with purple, and the inner surface a lime green to light purple, with purple veins. Found in bush clumps in lowveld regions.

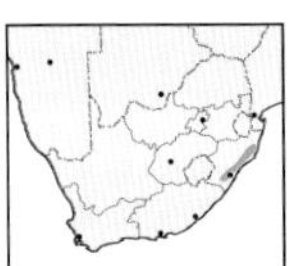

Ceropegia fortuita

Fortunate find ceropegia

Plants occur as twining climbers in scrub vegetation. From slightly flattened succulent tubers they produce a single, sparsely branched twining stem that climbs to about thigh height. The small leaves have short stalks and margins with only a few hairs. Flowers are produced during winter, each little bloom being only 3 cm long, with a swollen base, above which the thin tube extends, expanding to a purple-green, hairy cage. Difficult to distinguish from other ceropegias when not in flower. Found in hot, dry river valleys.

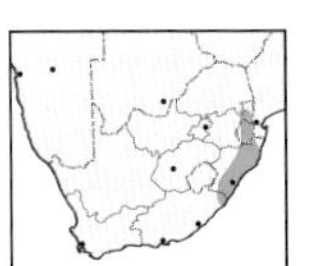

Ceropegia sandersonii

Giant ceropegia | *Sambreelblom*

This succulent vine climbs through shrubs and trees, sometimes reaching a height of 4 m. The simple, fleshy leaves are borne in pairs along the slightly warty stem. Flowers are large, up to 7 cm long and 2.5 cm wide across the mouth. The floral tube has a swollen base and a narrow neck and broadens to form a funnel-shaped mouth; this is capped with a wavy hood that is fringed with long, eyelash-like hairs. The creamy green hood is uniformly dotted light green; the outer tube is cream with longitudinal green stripes. Found in bushveld habitat.

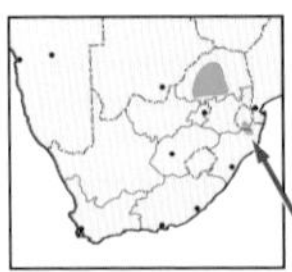

Ceropegia stapeliiformis subsp. *serpentina*

Serpent ceropegia | *Slangkambro*

Plants possess thickly succulent, warty stems that trail to form a snake-like mass on the ground, leaving the more slender, twining branches to climb through neighbouring scrub to the light. Here the peculiar flowers are produced, from the side resembling a gardening fork. Flowers during mid- to late summer. Unlike many of this species' relatives, the flowers are usually open at their apex. The lobes are free and do not spread. The floral tubes are cream, mottled purple to various degrees, while the outer lobe margins and apices are purple-brown. A multitude of hairs are evident along the lower lobe margins.

Ceropegia woodii

Necklace vine, String-of-hearts

The stems of this familiar hanging-pot subject usually trail downwards, although they may occasionally climb a little; along their length small tubers often form at the nodes. The heart-shaped leaves sometimes curve upwards along their margins, becoming spoon-like, so that they resemble miniature waterlily pads. The smooth, fleshy leaves are dull purple below and a uniform green above, although they may be mottled silvery green (variegated) on the upper surface. The small flowers, borne in mid- to late summer, are held upright. Each bloom has a swollen pink base that narrows along the tube before expanding again to produce a cage-like apex with five lobes joined at the tips. A profusion of dark purple hairs spills out between these 'bars'. Occurs naturally on cliff edges within forest situations, its small tubers embedded in soil banks or on rocky ledges.

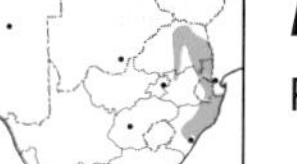

Huernia hystrix

Porcupine huernia

The succulent stems of this species are grey-green and form dense, ankle-high mats. Each stem is five-angled, with swollen projections (tubercles) that harden at their apex into a sharp, yellow spike. Flowers throughout the year, but mainly during summer. The flowers are presented either between the stems or off to the side of the clump and face upwards. Each bloom is about 5 cm across, and star shaped, although, often, some of the lobes will fold back behind the flower. The inner flower surface is covered with fleshy, pointed bumps up to 5 mm in length. Flowers vary considerably in their markings, even within populations, but they consistently possess maroon stripes, dots and dashes in concentric rings. Occurs in dry and hot situations, often at the edge of rock sheets in the light shade of grasses or other succulent species such as aloes.

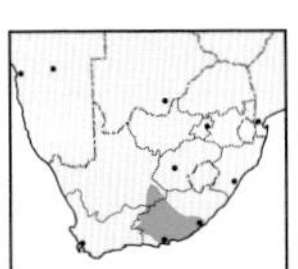

Huernia thuretti

Bitterghaap

Plants are low-growing, creeping succulents that consist of short, stubby stems. These stems are light green, distinctly angled, and carry numerous small, harmless protuberances along their entire length. Flowers are typical of those of most carrion flowers in that they are foul-scented and the colour of putrid flesh. Plants flower in summer. The species is widespread in the arid interior of the central Eastern Cape and parts of southern KwaZulu-Natal.

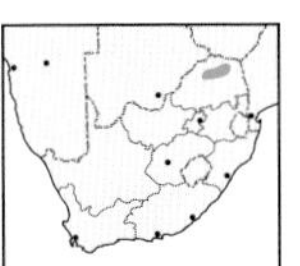

Huernia whitesloaneana

These miniature stem succulents grow in colonies. The purplish-green stems grow no taller than 3 cm, and are four- to five-angled with rounded projections (tubercles) along the ridges. Flowering occurs during mid-summer. The blooms face upwards when produced within the clump, but outwards if formed on the colony edge, for they find support on the ground. The tiny, bell-shaped flowers are only about 1 cm across and are cream, with maroon mottling. They are smooth on the outer surface but with minute, pimple-like bodies (papillae) on the inside. Though small, they still smell foul. Found wedged into the crevices of rock pavements, in exposed situations at altitudes above 1 000 m. Plants occur only in the Soutpansberg and Blouberg of Limpopo.

Huernia zebrina

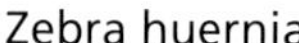

Zebra huernia

Plants are mat-forming stem succulents, with each stem five-angled and the approximate dimension of a finger. Stems are grey-green with purple mottling; the stem ridges possess sharply pointed tubercles, each of which is tipped with a hard, slender tooth. In late summer, plants produce star-shaped flowers about 5 cm across, which have a plastic appearance. These have a shiny, smooth, raised ring in the middle, which, usually, is predominantly maroon. The surrounding five corolla lobes are maroon striped on a cream background, and lightly hairy. Plants are found in stony and rocky areas, beneath shrubs and trees in dry woodland.

Ischnolepis natalensis

Propeller vine

Also known as *Petopentia natalensis*. Plants are more conspicuous by their tubers than their climbing stems and glossy paired leaves. Within its range this species is not uncommonly encountered growing along well-drained cliff ledges with its silver-brown tubers dangling in connected groups, fully exposed. Though potato-shaped, they are considerably larger. The moderately succulent leaves are dark green with purple veins and a prominent raised mid-rib on the underside. Along the red-brown stems yellow-green flowers appear in small clusters, the lobes of each flower spreading back on maturing, and sometimes twisting propeller-like in the middle. Each petal has a central red stripe on its underside. Blooms are produced between early spring and mid-autumn. Fruits are paired pods.

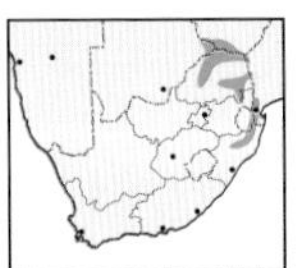

Orbea carnosa subsp. *keithii*

Plants often form large clumps on stony ground. The broad, succulent stems are four-angled, grey-green in colour with purple mottling, and are usually about 10 cm tall. Long, rounded projections (tubercles) are found along the stem ridges. Small, bell-shaped flowers of up to 2 cm in diameter appear in late summer. These thick, fleshy blooms are maroon-brown with white spots on their warty and wrinkled upper surfaces. Found in the semi-shade in open woodland, or fully exposed in shallow soil pockets that overly granite domes.

Orbea lutea subsp. *lutea*

Geelaasblom

Plants are low-growing. Their short, stout stems are angled, light green, mottled with purple and adorned with pointed protuberances that resemble spines. Flowers are bright yellow and borne in clusters. The flowers have a very pungent smell, resembling that of putrid meat. This species tends to creep along the ground, rooting where the stems touch the soil. In this way plants 'move' to suitable areas, e.g. under shrublets, where they flourish and receive some protection from predators and harsh, direct sunlight. The species is widely distributed in central South Africa and Botswana.

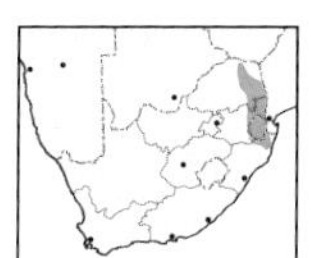

Pachypodium saundersii

Kudu lily | *Koedoelelie*

This is a pachycaul succulent, i.e. it has a grossly swollen stem base. It is squat and bears numerous branches of a much narrower diameter, which reach a height of 1 m. Each branch is set with very long, paired spines, and during the summer months produces somewhat keeled leaves along its length, with most leaves clustered towards the branch ends. The white flowers are produced during autumn and early winter and are about 5 cm across. The lobes have wavy margins and often slightly overlap. Fruits are twinned grey pods, speckled maroon. Grows in exposed, hot, dry and rocky areas.

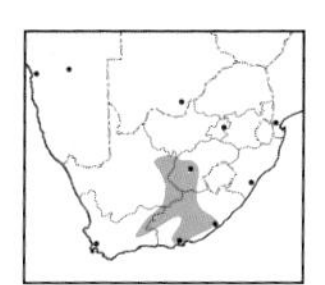

Pachypodium succulentum

Thickfoot | *Dikvoet*

Plants with a massive underground caudex (the expanded region at the junction of the stem and root), only the tip of which is exposed. From the silvery orange stem apex several erect branches are produced to a height of about 50 cm, each shoot bearing vicious orange spines in pairs. The dusty green leaves are stalkless with a prominent mid-vein below and the leaf margins rolled under. The terminally borne flowers are tubular for half their length, with five lobes peeling back; they vary from white to crimson and appear during spring. Found in stony grassland and along rock ridges.

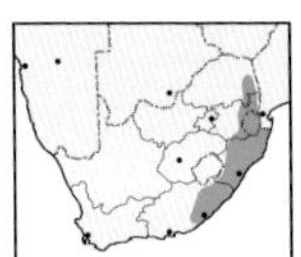

Raphionacme flanaganii

Flanagan's raphio

This tuberous-rooted species produces velvety, twining, brown stems with paired, lightly downy leaves. Despite the presence of these hairs, the leaves are quite shiny, resembling those of the familiar garden genus *Petrea*. The leaves are blue-green, with prominent yellow veins. Flowers are produced from early to mid-summer in small clusters at the nodes. Each bloom has five yellow lobes that are strongly curved backwards to reveal purple markings at their base, and a medusoid floral portion at their centre. Grows in valley bushveld and sand forest.

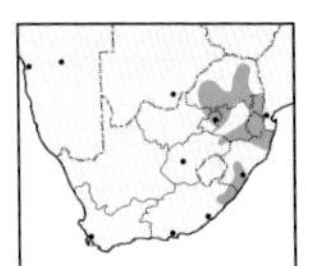

Raphionacme galpinii

Galpin's raphio | *Melkbol*

The underground tuber of this species may be partly exposed, depending on its location, and normally produces a single, erect stem. This bears velvety, egg-shaped leaves along its length and, from late spring through to mid-summer, a compact inflorescence of medium-sized flowers at its apex. Each flower is covered in silvery hairs on the outside, but opens to present a green-brown, smooth inner surface. Plants are found in rocky grassland, or on sheetrock expanses; in such situations they are associated with resurrection plants such as *Selaginella dregei*.

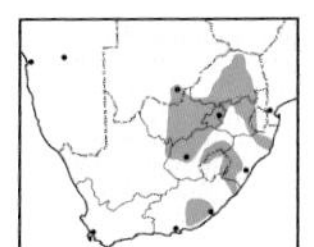

Raphionacme hirsuta

False gentian | *Khadiwortel*

The large, rock-shaped underground tuber produces many short, succulent branches, which bear either hairy or smooth, dark green leaves arranged on thin, short to medium-length stems. These give specimens the appearance of small shrubs. At the apices of these shoots, masses of gentian-purple flowers are borne, lightly hairy on the underside and smooth and waxy above. These usually appear before the leaves, or at least before they are fully expanded. The lobes of the crown-like structure (corona) in the flower centre are either purple or white; flowers appear from early spring through summer. A sun-loving species found in rocky grassland at a wide range of altitudes.

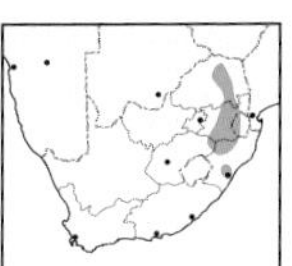

Riocreuxia picta

The rootstock is a cluster of long, succulent roots, from which the annual twining stems are produced, bearing heart-shaped leaves. This species may be readily recognised by the longitudinal purple or purple-brown veins that stripe the tubular flowers, each of which has a swollen base and five, narrow apical lobes joined cage-like at their tips. Upright flowers are produced in profusion during mid- to late summer. A plant of forest margins, this climber scrambles for several metres into surrounding low trees and scrub.

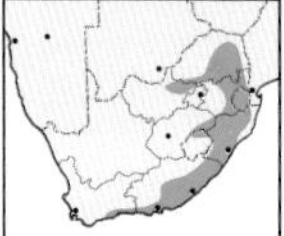

Riocreuxia torulosa

Candle vine | *Kandelaarblom*

A scrambling vine reaching a height of 5 m. The heart-shaped leaves vary greatly in size and hairiness. Up to three branched inflorescences are produced at some nodes, providing a mass display of lantern flowers. The flower colour varies tremendously, from an almost uniform cream with light green longitudinal stripes, to greenish-cream and yellow with light mauve stripes. Individual flowers have a swollen base that tapers above, before extending as an elongated cage-like structure. The twin pods are papery when mature, splitting to release a mass of fluffy seeds. Found scrambling through bush clumps and along forest margins.

Sarcostemma viminale

Caustic vine | *Melktou*

A succulent vine that drapes itself over neighbouring trees. The climbing stems are grey-green, without obvious leaves, and seemingly segmented, with branches forming at about 60 degrees to the node at which they are formed. At the ends of the lightly wrinkled stems, yellow-green star flowers are produced in small clusters, mainly during mid-summer, but at any other time of year too. All plant parts release sticky white milk when broken open. Found in hot bushveld and rocky outcrop regions.

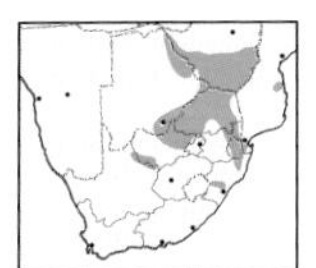

Stapelia gigantea

Giant stapelia | *Aasblom*

Plants comprise colonies of upright velvety stems some 20 cm tall; these stands may cover several square metres. Each blue-green stem is four-angled and highly branched. They are edged with small, blunt teeth. The very large, star-shaped flowers possess a distinctly wrinkled upper surface, and are creamy yellow and banded concentrically with many thin, maroon stripes. Blooms may attain a diameter of 40 cm. The upper flower surface is lightly hairy throughout, with much longer, fine hairs fringing the flower lobe margins. This combination of colours, coupled with the foul smell emitted by the blooms, serves to attract carrion flies as pollinators. This widespread species is usually found in the partial shade of arid bush clumps and on the edge of sheetrock.

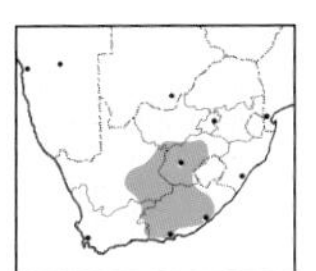

Stapelia grandiflora

Bobbejaankambro

Plants form small colonies of upright, four-angled, branching stems. These are edged with blunt, spine-tipped teeth. The flowers, which superficially resemble those of *S. gigantea*, are much smaller, attaining usually less than half of their diameter, at 10–15 cm. The wine-coloured upper surface of the flower is prominently wrinkled and hairier towards the base, with very long hairs adorning the corolla margins. Clumps of the grey-green stems of this stapeliad are to be found occasionally, tucked between rocks on hillsides, or growing in the light shade of trees in valley bushveld and the Karoo.

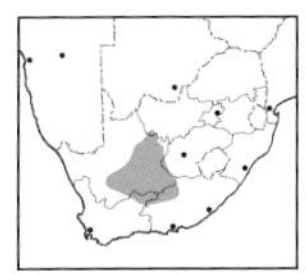

Stapelia olivacea

Plants comprise several upright, softly hairy and slender stems that reach 12 cm in length. They are four-angled, blue-green on the ridge edges and dark green to maroon in the grooves between, so appearing striped along their length. During late summer, star-like red-brown to olive green flowers are formed, each about 3 cm across and with a wavy upper surface and a fringe of long hairs. Plants form small clumps growing among rocks, often hidden by the karroid shrubs and grass tussocks in the shade of which they live. They are frequently associated with dolerite substrates at higher altitudes.

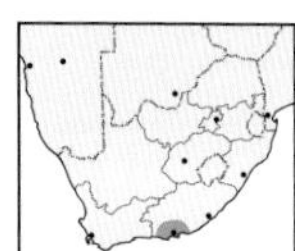

Aloe africana

Uitenhage aloe | *Uitenhage-aalwyn*

Plants grow as stately, mostly single-stemmed specimens that can reach a height of over 2 m when very old. The leaves are strongly recurved and concentrated in small clusters at the tips of the stems, from where they radiate in a haphazard fashion. Dried leaves remain on the stems for a long time. The inflorescences are tall and candle-like and carry numerous small, tightly packed flowers, the bottom-most ones typically turning upwards. This Eastern Cape species can flower at any time of the year, with a peak in winter.

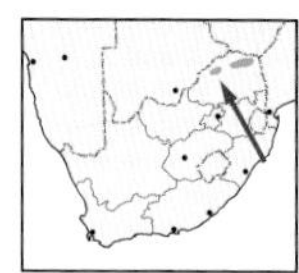

Aloe angelica

Soutpansberg aloe
Soutpansbergaalwyn

Very tall, single-stemmed trees with distinctive, aloe-like silhouettes. The stems are covered in the remains of dry leaves that wither away from the bottom to give plants a typically conical shape. Leaves are dark green, strongly recurved and are armed with short, brownish teeth. The elegantly recurved, yellow-orange flowers are quite long, but clustered into short, compressed inflorescences. This is a strikingly beautiful savanna aloe that flowers in winter. It is restricted to a small area of bushveld north of the Soutpansberg in Limpopo. The species is not as easy to cultivate as other more common tree-like aloes such as *A. ferox* and *A. marlothii*. Horticultural challenges may well be indicated by its restricted distribution range.

Aloe arborescens

Krantz aloe | *Kransaalwyn*

Plants grow as large clumps with numerous rosettes at the tips of the stems. Usually the stems are clothed in the remains of dried leaves. The leaves are thick, sickle-shaped and armed with fairly sharp, but generally harmless teeth. Leaf colour varies from blue-grey to bright green. The inflorescences are the shape of inverted cones and consist of a multitude of pencil-shaped flowers. Flower colour varies from crimson-red through orange to yellow. Plants flower in winter. The species is very widespread in the southern and eastern parts of southern Africa, particularly along the mild coastal belt.

Aloe barberae

Tree aloe | *Boomaalwyn*

The tallest of all the aloes, plants are robust trees up to 20 m tall. The stems are covered with thin, ash-grey 'bark' that is rough to the touch. Branches are usually once-branched and at maturity each one carries a small cluster of strongly recurved leaves. In young specimens the leaves are much longer and borne erectly. Dry leaves are soon shed, leaving the trunks and branches smooth. Leaf margins are armed with short, harmless, white teeth. The inflorescences are fairly short, but the large, orange flowers are carried in compact, cylindrical clusters. The species flowers in winter and spring. It occurs in forests and grassland along the eastern seaboard of South Africa, extending northwards into Mozambique.

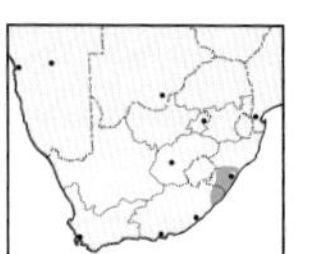

Aloe candelabrum

Candelabra aloe
Kandelaaraalwyn

These large, robust specimens remain unbranched. The leaves are thick with accumulated water, but tend to be more deeply channelled above and more strongly recurved than those of *A. ferox*, in which it is sometimes included. The lower parts of the trunks are clothed in the remains of dead leaves. Inflorescences are multi-branched and consist of several thick 'candles' that remain erect. These inflorescences are shorter than those of *A. ferox*. Flower colour is fairly consistently a dull reddish colour. The species flowers in mid-winter and has a restricted range in the KwaZulu-Natal midlands, particularly around Pietermaritzburg.

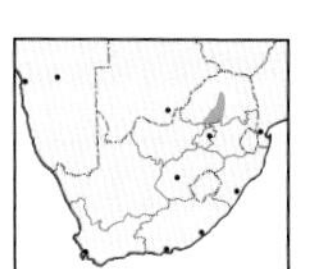

Aloe castanea

Cat's tail aloe | *Katstertaalwyn*

Plants usually grow as many-forked trees that carry a large canopy consisting of two or more rosettes perched on forked stems. These stems are covered in the remains of dry leaves. The leaves are a drab green and their margins are armed with short teeth. Small, yellowish-brown flowers are tightly packed in long inflorescences. Nectar is characteristically dark brown. The species flowers in winter. It occurs in the savanna regions of northern South Africa.

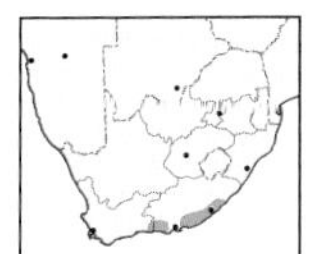

Aloe ciliaris

Climbing aloe | *Rankaalwyn*

Scraggly, climbing shrubs that consist of numerous stems arising from an underground rootstock. Leaves are flattened, tapering, and widely spaced on the stems. Each of the stem-clasping leaf bases is adorned with a fringe of soft, white, hair-like teeth. Large, bright red flowers with darker green tips are carried in short, dense racemes in winter. The species is a typical component of the Eastern Cape's thicket vegetation.

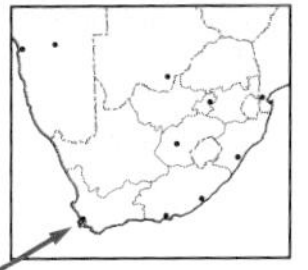

Aloe commixta

Fynbos aloe
Fynbosaalwyn

Plants consist of numerous, scraggly, leaning or creeping stems that arise from an underground rootstock. Leaves are flat, strongly tapering, and are adorned with short, whitish, marginal teeth. Flowers are bright yellow, quite large and carried in tight clusters on short, upwardly curved inflorescence stalks. Flowering takes place in late winter and spring. The species is restricted to a few localities in the extreme southwestern Cape, around Cape Town, and slightly beyond.

Aloe davyana

Spotted aloe
Bankrotaalwyn

Plants grow as solitary or, rarely, clump-forming specimens that remain soil-hugging. The usually short, fat leaves are packed in tight clusters that often do not protrude above the dense grasses among which they grow. The leaves typically die back from their tips in winter and turn a dusty, purplish-brown when they flower in the cold season. Inflorescences are multi-branched and carry large, pinkish-white flowers in mid- to late-winter. This species has a wide distribution above the climatically severe inland escarpment in east-central South Africa.

Aloe dichotoma

Quiver tree | *Kokerboom*

A medium-sized tree, usually with a single trunk. It carries a large canopy consisting of thick branches, each crowned with a rosette of short, fat, lance-shaped leaves. Dry leaves are soon shed. The trunk is beautifully adorned with a smooth, whitish or yellowish 'bark' that splits longitudinally to form sharp edges. Leaves are consistently a pale green colour. Flowers are bright yellow and borne in short, tight clusters from early to late winter. Occurs widely in the arid winter-rainfall area of South Africa and further north into Namibia.

Aloe excelsa

Noble aloe
Zimbabwe-aalwyn

Plants grow as tall, mostly single-stemmed specimens that can reach extraordinary heights. Low down the stems are devoid of leaves, but for most of their length they are covered by the remains of persistent, dry leaves. The erect, to slightly divided, dark green leaves are often generously covered in spines, and are carried on top of the stems. Small red or, rarely, yellow flowers are tightly packed in short, horizontally diverging inflorescences. Inflorescences are produced in late winter. This is a typical bushveld species from the far northeastern corner of South Africa, and beyond.

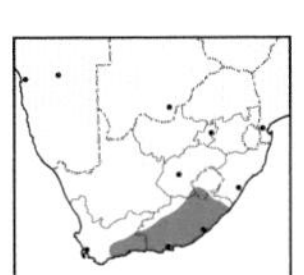

Aloe ferox

Bitter aloe, Karoo aloe | *Bitteraalwyn, Karoo-aalwyn*

Plants mostly grow as single-trunked specimens that can easily reach the height of a grown person. The trunks are topped with robust, many-leaved rosettes and clothed in the twisted, dry remains of the leaves. Leaves are thick and succulent and are borne erectly, or may be somewhat recurved. Marginal teeth are always present on the leaves, while some forms also have scattered teeth on both the lower and upper surfaces. In winter, erect, torch-like inflorescences carry fat, densely packed red, orange, yellow or white flowers that are thickly laden with nectar. The species is very characteristic of South Africa's Great and Little Karoo, where, in the dead of winter, it produces unforgettable displays usually of bright orange flowers.

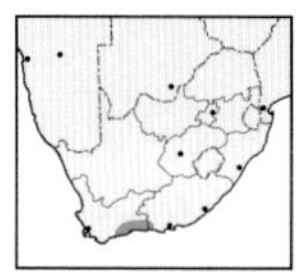

Aloe ferox × Aloe arborescens

Plants grow as shrubs that branch from the base into large, often tree-like specimens. Leaves are borne in dense rosettes and vary from vertically to horizontally disposed. Old, dry leaves remain on the stems. The leaf margins are armed with whitish prickles. Fat, tubular flowers are borne densely in thick, candle-like inflorescences. These 'candles' are carried in winter. This hybrid is very common where the two species co-occur, especially in coastal areas along the southern Cape.

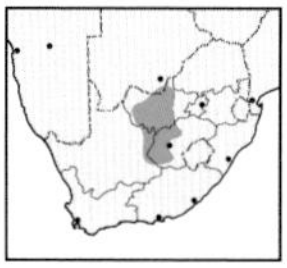

Aloe grandidentata

Karoo-bontaalwyn

Low-growing, rosulate leaf succulents that form very large, mound-shaped clumps of densely packed rosettes. Leaves are short, stubby, spotted white and invariably die back from the tips. Leaf margins are armed with short, very sharp brown teeth. Flowers are borne on multi-branched inflorescences and are a dull, reddish-pink. Unlike those of most species of spotted aloe, the flowers do not have a basal swelling, rather appearing distinctly club-shaped. The species flowers after mid-winter, into spring and even early summer.

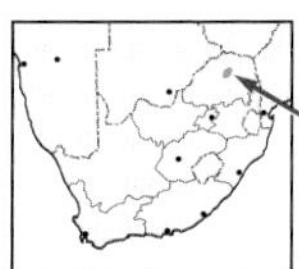

Aloe immaculata

These solitary, knee- to thigh-high specimens have fat, succulent leaves arranged in dense rosettes. Leaves are either uniformly dark green to brownish-green or may be adorned with numerous H-shaped, creamy white spots. Inflorescences are branched and consist of many pencil-shaped flowers with basal, bulb-like swellings. Flowers vary in colour from pink and peachy-orange to bright red. The inflorescences are produced in mid-winter. This species occurs in typical bushveld vegetation, in northern South Africa.

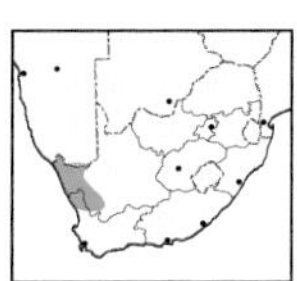

Aloe krapohliana

Krapohl's aloe

Plants are mostly unbranched and develop short stems that remain clothed in the remains of old, dry leaves. Leaves are bluish-green and distinctly cross-banded with lighter and darker green sections. Flowers are quite large and fairly densely packed into short racemes that are produced from mid- to late winter. This aloe is confined to a narrow strip on South Africa's winter-rainfall West Coast.

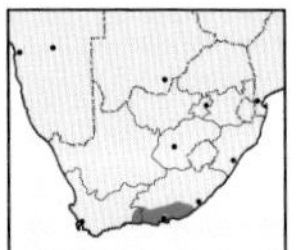

Aloe lineata var. *lineata*

Lined aloe | *Streepaalwyn*

Medium-sized to tall shrubby plants that produce off-sets from the base and stem. Much of the lengths of the stems are covered in the remains of old leaves. The light bluish-green leaves have faint to distinct, closely spaced, reddish, longitudinal lines. Flowers are tubular and a light orange to reddish colour. In the upperparts of the baseball bat-shaped inflorescences, the buds are covered by large, overlapping floral bracts. Inflorescences are produced in mid- to late summer, when few other large aloes are in flower. The species occurs in the southern coastal areas of South Africa, and slightly beyond.

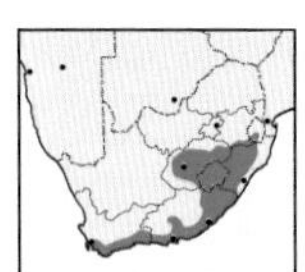

Aloe maculata

Common soap aloe | *Bontaalwyn*

Plants are solitary or suckering, and vary in size from small to medium-sized, with short, stout trunks. Leaves are recurved and densely marked with white, H-shaped spots, particularly on the upper surfaces. Leaf margins carry short, sharp, brownish teeth. Inflorescences are distinctly head-shaped and markedly flat-topped. The flowers are quite long, slightly curved inwards and consistently and prominently swollen at their bases. Their colour varies from a light pink to red, orange and yellow. Plants can flower at any time of the year, depending on their geographical origin. The species has a wide distribution from the Cape Peninsula eastwards and northwards.

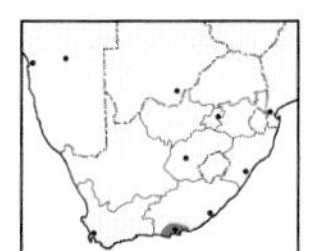

Aloe maculata × Aloe striata

Basteraalwyn

Plants are stemless, or short-stemmed, and rarely grow as individual rosettes. They typically form medium-sized, dense clusters. Leaves are boat-shaped and bear small, harmless teeth on a pink margin. Flowers are orange-pink and carried in head-shaped clusters, mostly in winter. This hybrid, which is very widely cultivated in domestic gardens, occurs naturally in some areas where the distribution ranges of the parents overlap and flower simultaneously, particularly in the Eastern Cape.

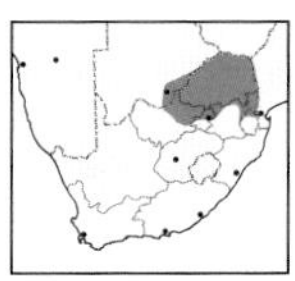

Aloe marlothii

Mountain aloe | *Bergaalwyn*

Large, single-trunked specimens up to 2 m tall. In exceptional cases, very old specimens can reach 8 m. The stems remain erect and the portion below the rosette is clothed in the gnarled remains of dry leaves. The many branched inflorescences remain horizontal, while the red, orange or yellow flowers are carried vertically on them. Plants often grow in dense clumps – in winter, entire hills will take on a yellowish hue when the species flowers. This aloe occurs in South Africa's savanna vegetation.

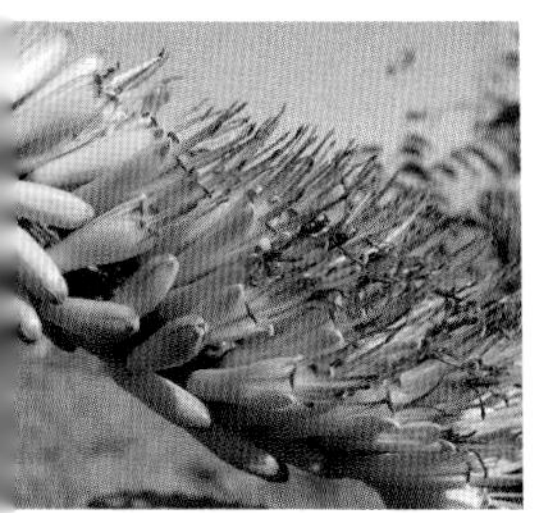

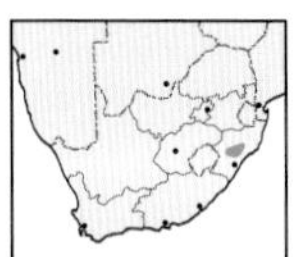

Aloe saundersiae

Only a few centimetres tall, these aloes usually grow singly or in small groups. They are stemless with the leaves sprouting directly from the ground, upwards and outwards in the shape of an egg cup. Leaves are narrow, not very succulent, tapering to a point, and adorned with minute, whitish, marginal teeth. The inflorescences have thin, erect stalks. Flowers are dull pink, quite large and are carried in small, but tight clusters. Flowering takes place in late summer and early autumn. The species is restricted to a few locations in the KwaZulu-Natal midlands, where it is considered to be endangered.

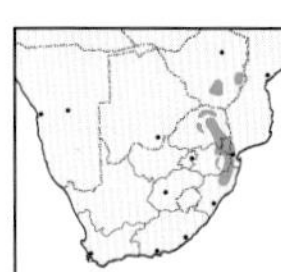

Aloe spicata

Spike aloe | *Laeveld-aalwyn*

Plants mostly grow as solitary or once-branched specimens. Their short trunks are clothed in the skirt-like remains of dried leaves. The leaves are a dull, light green colour, sharp-tipped, and adorned with short, brown prickles on their margins. Inflorescences resemble cat's tails and carry numerous small, yellow, cup-shaped flowers. They harbour large quantities of dark brown nectar, which attracts birds and insects. Plants flower in winter and are generally restricted to the eastern escarpment of the Drakensberg, towards the lowveld.

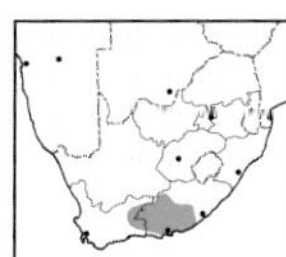

Aloe striata

Coral aloe | *Koraalaalwyn*

Plants are low-growing and often have short, stout, creeping stems that are clothed in the decaying remains of the soft leaves. Leaves are a sea-green colour and lack teeth on their margins. Instead, they have bright pink margins. The inflorescences are multi-branched, but flat-topped. Flowers are short and bright orange. They have indistinct basal swellings, signifying a relationship with the true spotted aloes, which have fat-based flowers. The species flowers in spring and occurs in South Africa's Eastern Cape.

Aloe succotrina

Scree aloe | *Bergaalwyn*

Solitary or branched, robust shrubs that consist of numerous, lance-shaped, tapering leaves carried erectly. The leaves are papery and purple when dry. Their margins are armed with small, triangular, white teeth. The inflorescences are produced in late winter and shaped like inverted cones. Flowers are deep red. The species occurs on the Cape Peninsula and slightly beyond in the southwestern Cape mountains.

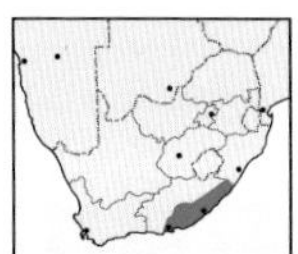

Aloe tenuior

Fence aloe

Scraggly, bushy shrubs consisting of numerous, thinnish stems that invariably lean to one side and eventually flop over under their own weight. Leaves are flat, lance-shaped and tend to be concentrated in the upper half of the stems. In very cold areas, plants are deciduous with even the stems dying off. In spring these resprout from ground level. Small yellow, red or orange flowers are carried in simple or, rarely, once-branched inflorescences. Flowers can be produced at any time of the year, particularly if plants are grown in mild areas. The species occurs mainly in the thicket vegetation of the Eastern Cape.

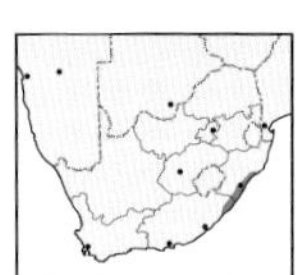

Aloe thraskii

Strand aloe | *Kusaalwyn*

Plants grow as large, single-trunked specimens. Their stout trunks are topped with large rosettes consisting of deeply channelled leaves. Leaf margins are consistently armed with short, sharp teeth, but, especially in mature plants, spines are absent from the lower and upper surfaces. The inflorescences are produced in winter, are quite short, and are thickly congested with small, fat, tubular flowers that vary from yellow to light orange. This is a typical coastal species and is often encountered within a few metres of the breaking waves on South Africa's mild, subtropical east coast, near Durban.

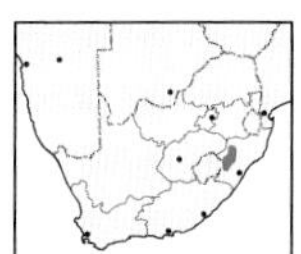

Aloe vanrooyenii

Van Rooyen's aloe

Solitary, stemless, or very short-stemmed, rosette-forming leaf succulents. Leaves are fairly short, somewhat triangular and carry white, H-shaped spots on both surfaces. Margins are armed with sharp, brown teeth. Flowers are arranged in multi-branched inflorescences and have the distinctive basal swelling characteristic of spotted aloes. Flowers are either orange or red. The dull green fruits characteristically grow to the size of golf balls. This is the only spotted aloe from KwaZulu-Natal that regularly flowers in summer.

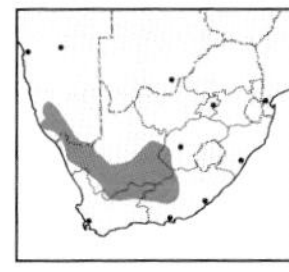

Aloe variegata

Partridge-breasted aloe

Kanniedood

Plants usually grow singly, or in small clumps, under little karroid shrublets, where they remain protected from the harsh rays of the sun. The dark green to dirty brown, white-mottled leaves are triangular in cross-section and have white, bone-like margins, but do not carry teeth. Short, stout inflorescences bear several loosely arranged, curved, tubular flowers in late winter or spring. The fruits are quite big for such a small plant, and the seeds carry large, papery, white wings to aid their dispersal by wind. The species occurs over a vast area above the climatically severe inland escarpment, particularly in the Little and Great Karoo. Leaves of the species are very reminiscent of those of *Gasteria* species.

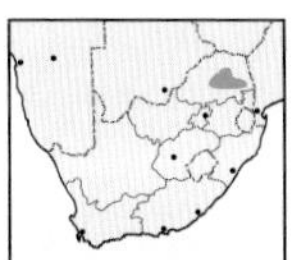

Aloe wickensii

Plants form tidy, stemless rosettes that carry numerous erect or slightly spreading leaves. The leaves are dull to yellowish-green and have short, sharp teeth on their margins. Leaf surfaces tend to be slightly rough to the touch. Variously coloured, pencil-shaped flowers are borne on branched inflorescences. In *A. wickensii* var. *lutea* flower colour is a uniform yellow. Plants can flower as early as February and as late as August, with a peak in mid-winter. The species occurs widely in the savanna of northern South Africa.

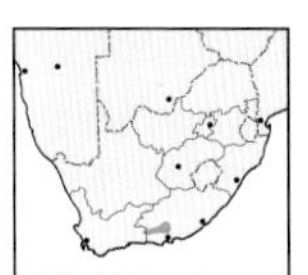

Astroloba deltoidea

Kleinaalwyn

Plants produce numerous erect, tightly arranged stems that can reach knee height. The stems are densely covered in small, very sharp-tipped, triangular leaves that point upwards. Curiously, leaves tend to die back haphazardly along the stems as the plants mature. The leaves have a lighter green to white margin. Flowers are carried in a lax, open inflorescence. The flowers are small, greenish-white and do little to enhance the explorer's ability to locate the plants in the veld. This species from the arid Eastern Cape interior flowers in summer.

Bulbine frutescens

Bulbinella | *Geel kopieva*

Plants are low-growing shrublets that occur singly or can form small, but dense mats. Stems and branches are thin, somewhat woody, brittle and carry leaves along their lengths. The leaves are thin, soft and pointed. Bright yellow or orange flowers are loosely arranged on thin inflorescences. The flowers are star-shaped with spreading, separate petals and characteristically support feathery stamens (male reproductive organs). Flowers can be produced at any time of the year. The species has a vast distribution range in South Africa, particularly in thickets and the Karoos. The soothing juices contained in the leaves are used to treat burns and skin conditions.

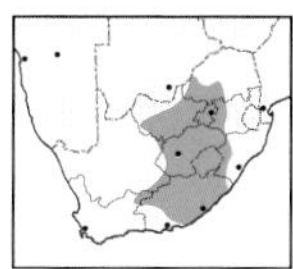

Bulbine narcissifolia

Bulbine | *Geel kopieva*

These low-growing, bulb-like shrublets have the distinct appearance of a narcissus or other bulbous plant. Leaves are flat and somewhat tongue-shaped, but still unmistakably succulent. Leaf colour varies considerably, from blue-green to a pleasant light green. Inflorescences are quite robust, congested and densely flowered. The flowers are bright yellow. The filaments carrying the male reproductive organs in the flowers are distinctly bearded and appear feathery. Plants tend to flower at any time of the year if watered in a garden, but in their habitat flower in spring and early summer. The species has a very wide geographical distribution range in the arid grasslands of South Africa.

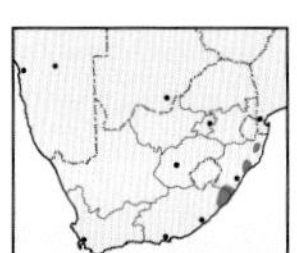

Bulbine natalensis

Broad-leaved bulbine | *Geel kopieva*

Plants consist of flat, tapering leaves that are carried in aloe-like rosettes. The leaves also look like those of typical aloes, but they are much softer in texture and do not have any marginal, or other, spines. The leaves partly die back, yielding reddish-brown, papery tips. The inflorescences are elongated and appear feathery, especially when young, because the long bracts that support the flowers exceed the length of the buds. The flowers, borne during spring and summer, are bright yellow and are carried in a fairly dense arrangement around a central, unbranched inflorescence stalk. They have bearded filaments. Wilted flowers characteristically turn deep brown. The species occurs in the mild coastal areas of the eastern seaboard.

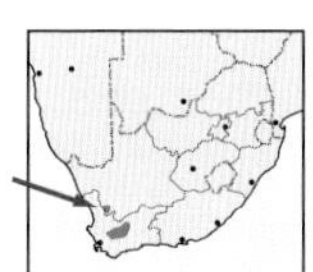

Bulbine succulenta

Compass plant

Plants are low-growing rosettes consisting of fat, thick leaves that are carried erectly. The leaves clasp the stems and are very soft in texture. In the dry summer months, characteristic of its habitat, the plant's leaf tips typically die back, giving them a blunt appearance. Inflorescences are borne in spring and considerably exceed the height of the rosettes. The flowers have bearded filaments, are bright yellow, and are fairly dense on the inflorescence stalk. The species is restricted to the winter-rainfall region of the Western Cape.

Gasteria acinacifolia

Bosaalwee

An aloe-like plant with large, single rosettes that are well hidden in its habitat. The leaves are densely spotted, distinctly angled and have sharp, bone-like margins. In summer, this species produces a flat-topped inflorescence, which carries numerous horizontal branches. The flowers are brightly coloured, very large and typically dangle from the branches. Plants are found concealed among dune scrub. The species is restricted to a narrow strip along South Africa's Eastern Cape coast.

Gasteria batesiana

Plants grow as small clusters of tightly packed rosettes. Leaves are tongue-shaped, very fat, and most commonly have a very rough surface, even though forms with smooth leaves are known. Large, elongated flowers that are a combination of dull red and light green are carried widely spread along inflorescence branches that tend to grow out sub-erectly to horizontally from the rosettes. The species occurs in KwaZulu-Natal and Mpumalanga.

Gasteria croucheri subsp. *pendulifolia*

Bosalwee

Plants have long, pendulous leaves arranged in a rosette. The smooth leaves are relatively narrow and, at times, ribbon-like. During spring, simple or branched inflorescences (often branched in larger plants) droop from the rosette. These bear a row of hanging, tubular flowers, each slightly constricted in the middle, pink towards the base and creamy white above. Plants grow on sandstone cliffs in the greater Durban area, typically on the cooler, south-facing aspects and often in the partial shade of surrounding vegetation.

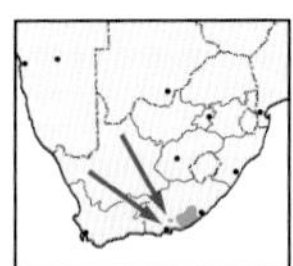

Haworthia cymbiformis

Plants consist of several small, aloe-like rosettes that slowly cluster to form medium-sized, ball-shaped clumps. Leaves are a near-translucent light green, boat-shaped and very soft, easily becoming damaged. The small, two-lipped flowers are a brilliant white and loosely packed on an elongated, wiry stalk that can appear at any time of the year. A cliff-dwelling, Eastern Cape thicket species, it grows well in semi-shade, where its soft leaves are protected against the harsh rays of the South African sun.

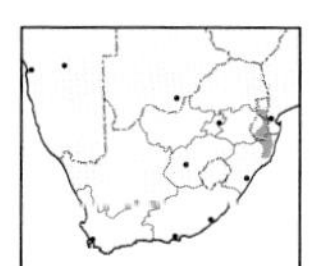

Haworthia limifolia var. *limifolia*

Fairy washboard

Plants are slowly clump-forming and grow as small to medium-sized clusters of little aloe-like rosettes. Leaves are pointed, light to dark green and typically adorned with white or green cross bands, giving them a file-like appearance. Flowers at any time of the year, especially in cultivation. Inflorescences are usually unbranched, thin and wiry, and carry numerous small, white flowers that are loosely packed. Like most haworthias the flowers are distinctly two-lipped. The species occurs in the eastern parts of KwaZulu-Natal and slightly beyond, even in Mozambique and Swaziland.

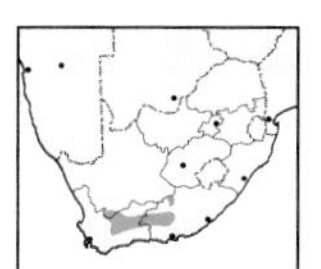

Haworthia viscosa

Koedoekos

Plants grow in small to very large clumps that eventually dwarf the karroid shrublets under which they grow. Individual stems can become quite long, but are more typically only a few centimetres. Leaves are short, stubby, triangular in cross-section and sharp-tipped. Small, two-lipped, off-white flowers are carried loosely on thin, wiry inflorescences. The species is restricted to the arid karoo.

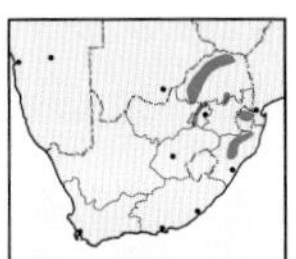

Kleinia fulgens

Coral senecio | *Koraalsenecio*

Low-growing shrubs that bear thick stems around which pairs of oval-shaped leaves with marginal indentations are carried. Leaf colour varies from dull green-grey to bluish-grey. A multitude of tiny, bright red florets are borne in tightly packed, head-shaped inflorescences that appear from April to September. The apices of the thinly tubular florets are star-shaped, giving the inflorescences a fluffy, tufted appearance. Each seed is adorned with a tuft of short, radiating white hairs. The species occurs in savanna vegetation in northern South Africa.

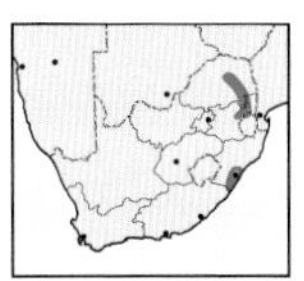

Kleinia galpinii

Small shrubs with oval- to spoon-shaped leaves attached to brittle stems that grow as thick as an adult's thumb. Stems are smooth and creep along the ground, becoming quite long. Lower down on the stems, faint scars show where leaves have been shed. Leaves are a dusty, dull grey-green and the margins are smooth. In contrast, the leaf margins of the similar-looking *K. fulgens* are usually bluntly toothed. From summer through to early winter small, bright orange flowers are borne in tight, head-shaped inflorescences. As is the case with many succulent daisies, the inflorescences of *K. galpinii* lack the distinctive ray florets usually associated with members of the Asteraceae. However, the striking orange colour of the disc florets more than makes up for the absence of the ray florets. The species occurs in northern South Africa, in savanna vegetation. The plant is an excellent landscaping subject as it grows easily from stem cuttings placed directly in the soil. Although preferring full sun, plants will tolerate dappled shade under trees.

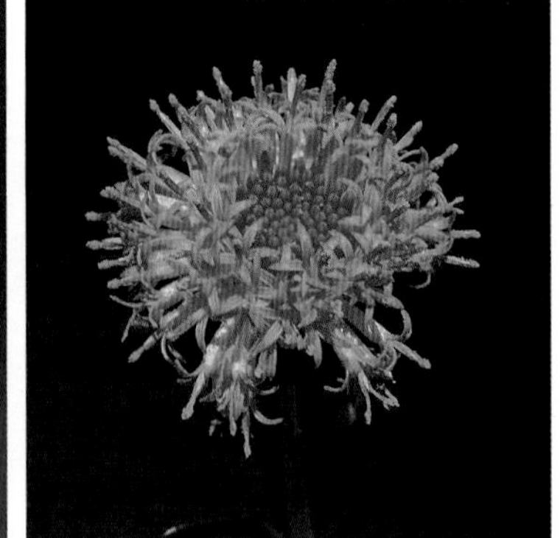

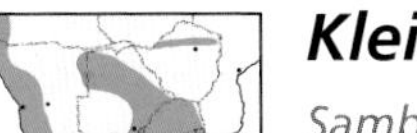

Kleinia longiflora

Sambokbos

Plants consist of dense tufts of thin, pencil-shaped, segmented stems that mostly remain erect, but may flop over sideways, especially on the edges of the clusters. The stems are dusty, light green and faintly striated lengthwise. The small, bract-like leaves are short-lived, giving the plant a euphorbia-like appearance. Dull, creamy white flowers are clustered into tight, head-shaped inflorescences. Inflorescences appear mostly from May to October. This savanna species has a wide distribution in northern and central southern Africa.

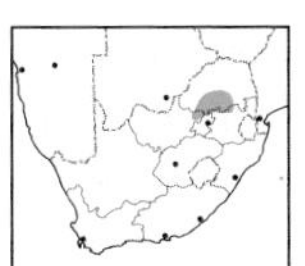

Kleinia stapeliiformis

Plants grow as small clumps of erect, finger-like stems that closely resemble those of carrion flowers (stapeliad members of the family Apocynaceae). The brownish-green stems appear thorny, but the short, stout protuberances that occur on the stem angles are quite harmless. Small, head-shaped inflorescences carry numerous tiny, bright red florets. These appear at the tips of the stems from late winter to early summer. The bright red flower clusters make it easy to detect the plants where they often grow in the shade of savanna shrubs and trees. The species occurs in northern South Africa in savanna vegetation.

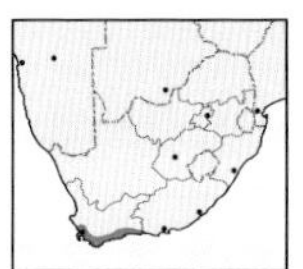

Othonna dentata

Plants are shrubby to knee height, with succulent stems and leaves. Superficially resembles a *Cotyledon* or arborescent *Crassula*, with leaves clustered at the tips of the long, silver-brown branches. The blue-grey leaves are arranged in spiral rosettes rather than paired as in *Cotyledon* or *Crassula*. Leaves are without a distinct leaf stalk, being wedge-shaped at the base and attached by the point. They have a red margin that is coarsely toothed, particularly along the upperparts. Leaves are egg-shaped, though broader in their upper half. Medium-sized, yellow daisy flowers are presented in loose inflorescences during spring. Found growing on cliff faces or exposed among rocks in the Western Cape.

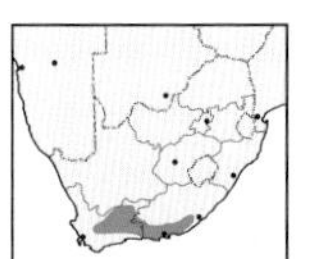

Senecio articulatus

Candle plant

Shin-high succulents that form strings of sausage-like stem sections, which break apart at the joints to spread vegetatively. The stems are light grey-green with darker green arrowhead markings peaking below the base of each leaf stalk. The succulent leaves are deeply incised and lobed, and blue-green in colour. Plants become deciduous during drought periods. The creamish-yellow flowers are produced during the summer months and possess a distinctly musty and often unpleasant scent. Plants may be found growing beneath bushes in the Karoo, and in valley bushveld in the Eastern Cape.

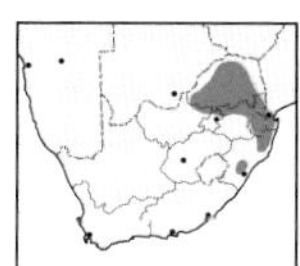

Senecio barbertonicus

Succulent bush senecio

Large shrubs or even small trees consisting of a single stem that branches low down and then re-branches higher up to yield a relatively rounded canopy. Leaves are light green, pencil-shaped and carried more or less erectly.

Flowers are bright yellow and tightly clustered into small, head-shaped inflorescences. The species has a long flowering season, from mid-winter through to mid-summer. It is widespread in the eastern and northern parts of South Africa, and is often found on krantz edges.

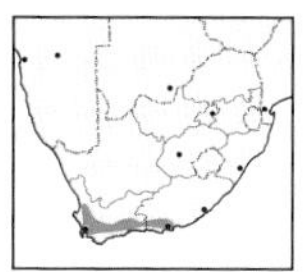

Senecio crassulaefolius

Sprawling shrublets that tend to topple over, especially in shady or very wet situations, to creep along the ground. The stems are the same sea-green as the leaves, which are pencil-shaped and usually fat with accumulated water. Flowers are a dull, creamy colour, packed into tight, head-shaped inflorescences and lack the usually brightly coloured ray florets so often associated with daisies. Inflorescences appear from

August to December. This is essentially a karroid species from the Western and Eastern Cape; but it also ventures into fynbos in some areas. It is a very useful species in domestic gardening as plants root easily from stem cuttings and can tolerate quite a bit of shade, which makes it worthwhile for planting under trees. If planted on a slope, these knee-high, blue-leaved shrubby bushes create a waterfall-like effect.

Senecio medley-woodii

Wood's senecio

Plants form well-branched shrubs, usually attaining thigh height, but may sometimes be found growing chest high. The stems are purple-red and covered with matted, downy hairs, becoming hairless with age. The greyish-green leaves are also felted, particularly on their undersides; they are thickly succulent and coarsely toothed along their upper edges. The large, bright yellow flowers are presented during winter, upturned on long stalks. The fruits are heads of fluffy wind-dispersed seeds. Usually found under krantz-edge scrub, which may constrain its growth. Also seen dangling on cliff ledges along major watercourses, or exposed on granite outcrops along the eastern seaboard.

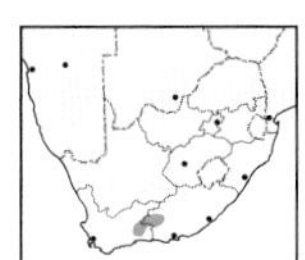

Senecio muirii

Small shrublets with thin, creeping to slightly erect stems. The flattened, but succulent leaves are oval-shaped and light green with longitudinal lines. Flowers are carried in small, head-shaped inflorescences that lack the usually brightly coloured ray florets of most daisies. The disc florets are creamy white and quite fine, but have distinctly recurved tips, giving the flower clusters a frilly appearance. The species occurs in the Western and Northern Cape, and flowers from March to April.

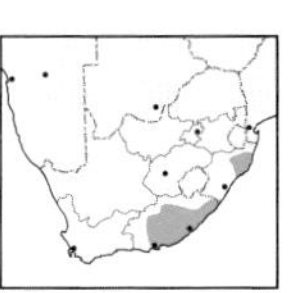

Senecio oxydontus

Plants are shrubby, reaching about knee height. The succulent, olive-green leaves possess distinctive petioles, which may be reddish in colour. Leaf margins are toothed along the upper two-thirds. Bright yellow daisy flowers, each with five to seven ray florets, are produced in small inflorescences. These are presented on long stalks above the plants from mid-summer through to winter. Occurs on rocky outcrops, cliff faces and krantz edges near forest margins in the Eastern Cape and KwaZulu-Natal.

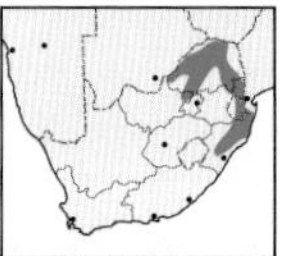

Senecio pleistocephalus

Plants are scandent – climbing without tendrils – their long stems trailing through, and over, the surrounding vegetation, sometimes smothering their support. The light green, succulent leaves are produced towards the ends of the creamy brown stems, each with a short petiole and coarsely serrated margin. Leaves are narrowly elliptic in outline and tend to fold upwards along their mid-rib. Dense terminal heads of orange-yellow flowers appear in winter, each daisy flower lacking ray florets, and are pleasantly honey-scented. Found in bushveld regions where it grows exposed on the margins of bush clumps and on rocky hillsides.

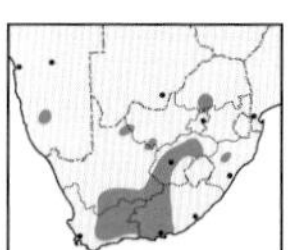

Senecio radicans

Baboon toes | *Bokbos*

Plants form string-like, creeping stems, which root along their length to form mats, or dangle from rock ledges. The small, succulent leaves are highly variable in shape, sometimes spindle- or banana-shaped, becoming redder when exposed to very bright light. They are well spaced along the trailing stem, and often point upwards, seemingly in a single row. Fragrant, solitary, pale mauve or white flowers are produced through most of the year, with flowering peaking during autumn and winter. This species prefers dry karroid veld where it occurs under rock ledges or bushes and forms matted colonies.

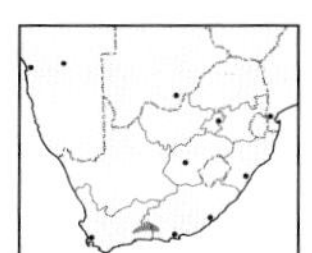

Senecio rowleyanus

String-of-pearls

Occurs as a clump of thin, wiry stems that carry pea-sized, globular, widely spaced leaves. The leaves are bright green and have a distinct translucent window along one side. Small, head-shaped inflorescences carry a multitude of tiny, off-white flowers. In their native karroid habitats, plants occur in the shade of fine-leaved shrublets. The species appears to be restricted to the Little Karoo. Although the inflorescences lack the bright colours associated with most daisy ray florets, it makes a very good subject for growing in hanging baskets in shady spots on patios.

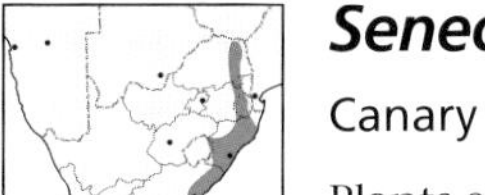

Senecio tamoides

Canary creeper | *Kanarieklimop*

Plants are scrambling, twining creepers that grow and flop onto surrounding plants. The leaves are heart-shaped to triangular in outline, flattened but distinctly thickened, and a shining dark green. Inflorescences consist of both ray and disc florets that are bright yellow. These are produced from spring, through summer, to early winter. This *Senecio* species has a wide distribution range in the essentially frost-free eastern parts of South Africa, in the Eastern Cape, KwaZulu-Natal, Mpumalanga, Limpopo, and Swaziland.

Begonia homonyma

Large-leaved wild begonia
Wildebegonia

Plants grow to waist height, retiring to their caudex over winter and resprouting in spring. The combination of large, nearly entire leaves and a succulent silvery brown and grossly swollen stem base (caudex) separates this species from other local begonias. This irregularly shaped caudex can attain a breadth of some 15 cm. Separate male and female flowers are produced on the same plant, the male flowers appearing usually before the female ones, albeit on the same inflorescence. Flower colour varies from white through to pink, with an obvious splash of yellow at their centre marking the presence of anthers or a stigma. Found on shady cliffs and forest banks in situations that are well drained and very dry during the winter months. Known only from the Eastern Cape and KwaZulu-Natal.

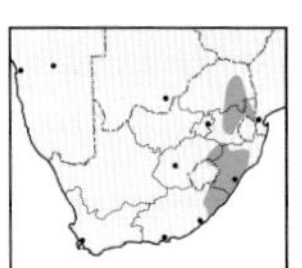

Begonia sutherlandii

Wild orange begonia | *Sutherlandbegonia*

This species has highly branched pink-orange stems that are produced annually from a perennial flattened tuber. Plants are usually found in large colonies. This widespread begonia generally has leaves that are entire, with irregular serrations along the margins. To show the degree of leaf shape variation a form from Inanda (Durban) with highly divided leaf blades is featured too (below right). As with all begonias, the leaf base is asymmetric. Separate male and female flowers are produced on the same plant, both a rich orange that brightens the shady forest habitat in which these plants grow. Plants can be found in moist soil or clinging to rock faces close to drip lines or waterfalls.

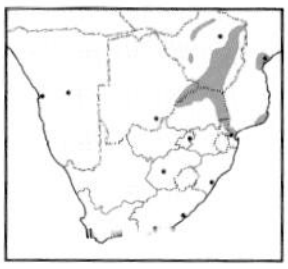

Adansonia digitata

Baobab | *Kremetart*

Massive trees that can reach an immense girth. The bark of these imposing trees looks like molten candle wax that has dried to create deep furrows and lumps. The leaves are bright, shiny green, especially when the first summer rains arrive. The very large, white flowers have a waxy appearance and are carried from early summer to autumn. Both flowers and fruit dangle from the canopy on long stalks. The fruit is furry and light green, and yields a pulp rich in nutrients. It is also a source of cream of tartar. Found in hot, dry lowveld regions in northern South Africa, and throughout many of the low-lying arid regions of Africa to the north.

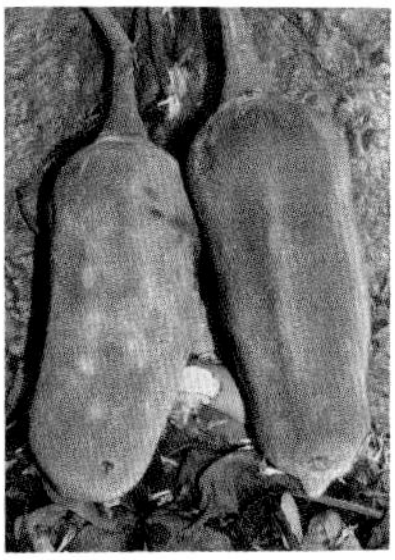

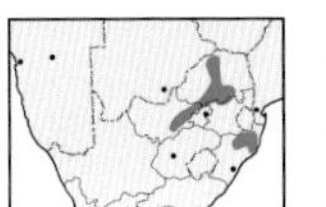

Cereus jamacaru Ⓐ

Queen of the night | *Nagblom*

Plants grow as large, organ-pipe-like stem clusters that consist of many vertical branches arising from a short main stem. The branches are deeply ribbed longitudinally and carry regularly spaced, small furry tufts from which very sharp, needle-like thorns arise. These small tufts also give rise to the large white flowers, borne in mid-summer, that open at night and are visited by fruit bats. The fruits can grow to the size of a tennis ball and are widely consumed by birds and mammals. This species, native to Brazil, has become an invasive weed, especially in southern Africa's bushveld, and should not be cultivated.

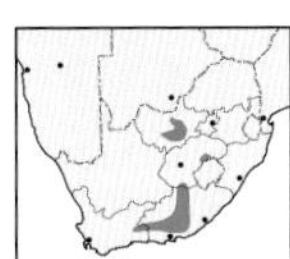

Echinopsis spachiana Ⓐ

Torch cactus | *Orrelkaktus*

Small to medium-sized clumps of erect, spiny stems that resemble those of some indigenous milkweed (*Euphorbia*) species. Stems are ribbed, light green and, although they usually remain erect, sometimes topple over, rooting along their entire length as they carry on growing. Flowers, produced in mid-summer to early autumn, are a striking creamy white colour and very large. They tend to open at night and are probably pollinated by bats or night-flying insects. Native to South America, the species has become invasive in large parts of South Africa's arid interior and should not be grown. Plants spread readily and easily take root.

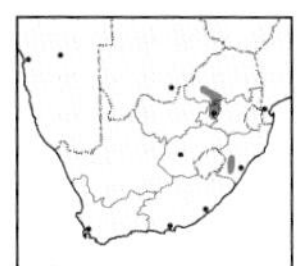

Harrisia martinii Ⓐ

Moon cactus | *Toukaktus*

Low-growing scramblers that thrive in the undergrowth below trees, forming impenetrable thickets. Stems resemble thick ropes and carry regularly spaced tufts of very sharp thorns along their length. Flowers are borne in late summer, open at night and become wilted by mid-morning the next day. The white flowers are replaced by bright red, golfball-sized fruits that split open when ripe to expose small black seeds in a white marshmallowy pulp. The species is very invasive in savanna and should not be cultivated.

Opuntia ficus-indica Ⓐ

Sweet prickly pear | *Boereturksvy*

Plants grow as robust shrubs or, more commonly, trees that consist of a short trunk supporting flattened, leafless pads. The pads, called cladodes, are bright green, oval-shaped and covered in sharp, needle-like spines. Each set of spines arises from a small, cushion-like structure called an areole. The short, bristle-like spines, or glochids, carried on the areoles are more menacing than the larger ones, as they are extremely irritating to exposed skin. The flowers, produced in summer, are orange or yellow and quite attractive. The fruit is delicious and widely eaten. Plants without spines are often cultivated in orchards for their fruit, and the pads are chopped up and fed to domestic livestock. This Mexican species is very weedy and invasive in many habitats and the spiny form should never be cultivated.

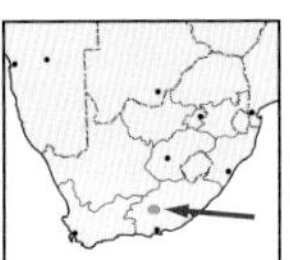

Opuntia microdasys Ⓐ

Bunny ears, Teddy bear cactus

Low-growing shrublets that consist of a network of pads that easily become detached and root where they fall. The light green pads lack the long, needle-like spines often associated with cacti, but are adorned with a multitude of cushion-like areoles that carry dense clusters of glochids that will severely irritate exposed skin. In some forms the glochids are dark brown or bright white. Flowers are bright yellow, and borne in summer. This Mexican species has a tendency to become invasive, especially the yellow form in South Africa, and should not be grown in gardens.

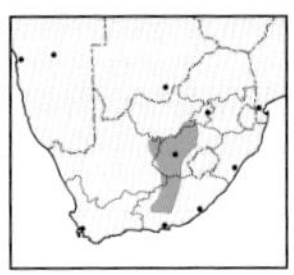

Opuntia robusta Ⓐ

Makturksvy

Plants grow as large, multi-branched specimens that consist of sizeable, round, flattened pads, strung together like pearls in a many-stringed necklace. The pads are light blue, the size of dinner plates and more or less spineless. Flowers are light yellow and mostly borne in early to mid-summer, on the margins of the pads. Fruits are quite large, a distinctive purple colour, and longitudinally grooved. The purple dye derived from the fruit has been used as a food colorant, for example in yoghurt. Plants of this Mexican species are often grown in orchards for fodder in times of drought and have escaped to become naturalised, especially in parts of South Africa's Free State and Eastern Cape provinces. Humans tend to prefer the fruit of *O. ficus-indica* to that of *O. robusta*.

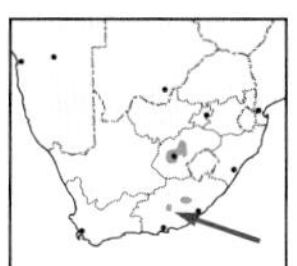

Opuntia spinulifera (A)

Saucepan cactus
Grootrondeblaarkaktus

Medium-sized to large shrubs that consist of several flattened pads strung together end-to-end. The pads are a drab light green colour and about the size of soup plates. Leaves are absent, but the pads are densely adorned with a combination of long, hair-like and shorter, white, needle-like spines. Flowers, borne in summer, are light yellow and give way to prickly, fig-like fruit. This Mexican species has invasive tendencies and should not be cultivated.

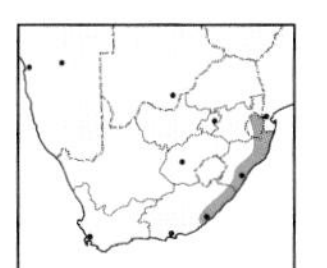

Rhipsalis baccifera subsp. *mauritiana*

Rope cactus | *Toukaktus*

Plants form pendulous clumps of thin, rope-like stems. These carry tiny, widely dispersed clusters of harmless, hair-like spines. Flowers are small, creamy white and rather insignificant. They are eventually replaced by small, white, near-translucent berries. Plants usually grow in the forks of tree branches or in the thin layer of soil in vertical rock cracks. This is the only cactus that is indigenous to South Africa, where it occurs along the east coast of KwaZulu-Natal to the Eastern Cape, and slightly inland.

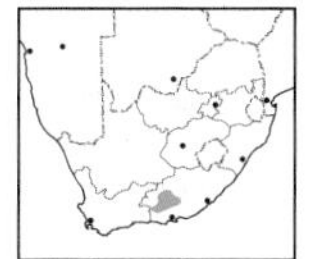

Tephrocactus articulatus (A)

Originating in Argentina, these low-growing plants consist of numerous, short, stubby stem segments that have a bumpy surface. Each little bump carries tufts of brown, bristle-like spines. Stems are dull green and segments easily become detached from one another. Flowers are creamy white and fairly insignificant, but in some forms the stems carry long, very flat, papery thorns that contribute to the popularity of the species in cultivation. Unfortunately, discarded plants easily root where they fall and the species has become invasive in the Karoo.

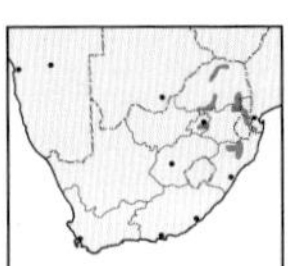

Cyanotis lapidosa

These small, rosette plants form a mat of densely arranged heads that somewhat resemble haworthias. The leaves are purplish-green and adorned with long, white hairs that are closely pressed to the leaf surfaces. The flowers, borne from mid-summer to autumn, are a pleasant purplish-mauve. Plants are typically shade-loving and usually hide under leaves dropped by trees, or in shady cracks in rocks. This is a typical savanna species.

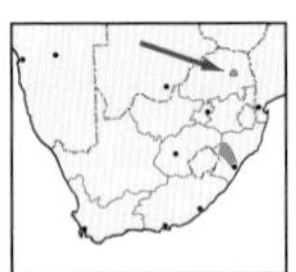

Cyanotis robusta

Plants to shin height with strap-like leaves clustered at the apex of a thick, vertical, underground rhizome. The leaves bear long white hairs below but are smooth above. From the base of the plant fertile shoots bearing flowers are produced; vertical at first, they become floppy with age. Along these purplish shoots are several nodes at which the inflorescences are borne. Each flower cluster is supported by a keel-like leaf, the individual bright purple-blue flowers resembling a doll's powderpuff with their densely hairy stamens. Flowers mainly during late summer. Plants may be found in grassland at the edge of bush clumps, or in dense colonies on rock sheets in full sun. Part of a confusing complex of unresolved species.

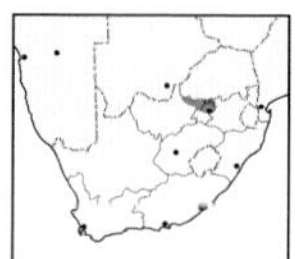

Adromischus umbraticola subsp. *umbraticola*

Small shrublets that carry dove's egg-shaped leaves on very short stalks. Leaves are fat, light grey-green and faintly mottled with tiny red blotches. Detached leaves easily strike root. The flowers are fairly small, tubular and carried on elongated stalks. Flower colour is deceptive, as the tips of the recurved petals are more intensely pinkish-white than the tube, which is pale green with an ash-grey bloom. This curiosity plant is best grown in small containers, as it favours rock cracks in its natural habitat. The species occurs in South Africa's inland grasslands, where it is never very common.

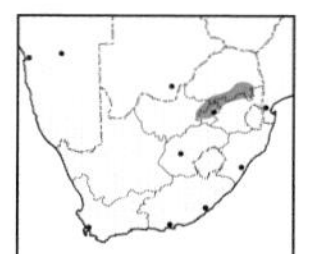

Bryophyllum delagoense Ⓐ

Mother of millions, Chandelier plant | *Kandelaarplant*

Plants grow as erect to leaning, fairly thin-stemmed shrubs. Leaves are pencil-shaped, cylindrical and an unremarkable dusty brown colour with darker, brownish-green blotches. Leaves, and the small plantlets they carry, become detached from the stems very easily and will strike root where they fall. Flowers are bright orange and carried in tight, head-shaped clusters at the tips of the stems in mid-winter. This Madagascan plant is a weed and tends to become invasive. It should not be cultivated.

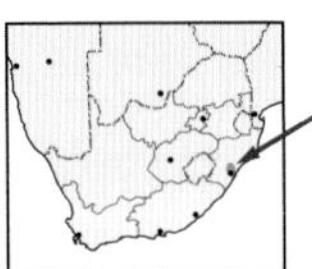

Bryophyllum proliferum Ⓐ

Plants grow as clump-forming shrubs reaching waist height. The succulent stems are square, and become quite woody with age. Each pair of pale green and thickly succulent leaves is arranged along the stem at right angles to the next; each leaf has three to five leaflets, each often with a purple margin, particularly under brighter light conditions. From along the edge of these leaflets, and also from the inflorescence branches, hundreds of tiny plantlets form, which drop off to root and grow at the base of the parent plant. During spring the open inflorescences are presented above the leafy plant portion; each flower has an open, box-like calyx, which is an inconspicuous green. From the apex of the flower the purple-tipped corolla protrudes, revealing its four lobes. Plants originating in Madagascar have escaped from cultivation in the greater Durban region, and may be found in disturbed situations both in shade and full sun. Alien invader; should not be cultivated.

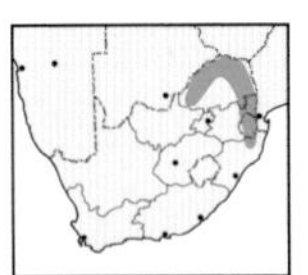

Cotyledon barbeyi

Bosveldplakkie

Plants mostly grow as many-stemmed, erect to leaning shrubs, which may attain a height of 3 m. The bottom-most part of each stem, which is as thick as an adult's finger, is devoid of leaves. The upper half of the stem carries widely spaced, very variably shaped, thick, succulent leaves that are most commonly oval in outline. Inflorescences, carried from autumn to late winter, are quite tall and loosely flowered. Flowers are distinctly swollen at the base and usually more intensely ruby red than are those of *C. orbiculata*. Found growing in the shade of bushveld clumps, or, more exposed, on rocky outcrops.

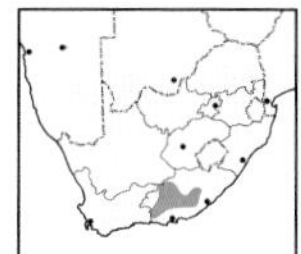

Cotyledon campanulata

Plants reach mid-shin height. The hairy leaves are thickly succulent, and near-cylindrical (almost banana-like and about finger-length), coloured light yellow-green, with a sharp to wavy reddish-brown apex. Each branch of the inflorescence bears three to eight yellow or yellow-green flowers, the petals of which open out widely, but never curve right back. Both the inflorescence stalk and the outer petal surfaces are slightly sticky. Flowers appear in mid-summer. This species is found in small colonies, growing in low karroid scrub, usually in valley bottoms.

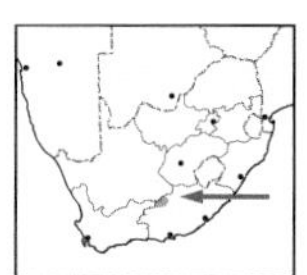

Cotyledon campanulata x *C. orbiculata*

Where both *C. campanulata* and *C. orbiculata* grow adjacent to one another, it is not uncommon to find hybrids forming in the veld. Their appearance is intermediate in most respects, including hairiness and shape of leaves, flower colour (varying from yellow to red), length of the floral tube, and the degree to which the petals open out. The inflorescence of such hybrids is usually sticky, a character inherited from *C. campanulata*. The form illustrated was found in Nieu Bethesda, growing in open karroid grassland.

Cotyledon orbiculata var. *orbiculata*

Pig's ears | *Plakkie*

Plants grow as thick-stemmed shrubs that carry fat, pencil- to oval-shaped or round and even-toothed leaves in opposite pairs. Leaf size and colour also vary considerably, but forms with nearly pure white, oval-shaped leaves are treated as belonging to the same species as those with dark green, soup plate-sized leaves. However, a number of different varieties are recognised. Inflorescences are fairly loosely flowered and flat-topped. Flowers are quite large and a dusty red to orange. Yellow-flowered forms are found less frequently. Flowers lack the basal swelling found in those of *C. barbeyi*. The flowering period stretches over several months, from March to December. This subspecies occurs widely across the arid western region of southern Africa.

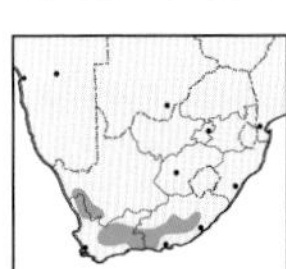

Cotyledon papillaris

Ranknenta

Found as small, low-growing colonies, each plant with close-packed leaves on short stems. One of the smallest members of its genus, its leaves sometimes have slightly lumpy surfaces with purple-brown tips. They may resemble miniature spindles. However, leaf shape can be highly variable between localities. During mid-summer the small inflorescences are presented well above the foliage. The corolla lobes of each pendulous flower are red to orange-red on their inside, revealing their bright colour as they spread right back. The long, greenish stamens appear to extend well beyond the mouth of the corolla tube once the petals have curved backwards. Plants grow at the base of karroid shrubs in light shade, occurring in habitats varying from succulent karoo to valley bushveld.

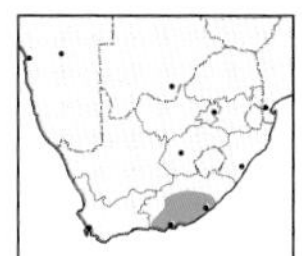

Cotyledon velutina

Succulent, strong-branching shrubs of this, the tallest member of the genus, can reach a height of 3 m, although plants normally grow to about chest height. The leaves are blue-green to greyish-brown and clustered towards the tips of the branches. They are oval with a pointed apex and purplish margins, and are often hairy. The bell-shaped flowers are borne in mid-summer on erect, purplish inflorescence stalks. Flower colour varies considerably from copper with yellow margins, to yellow-green with red margins. They occur in full sun or in the light shade of scrub.

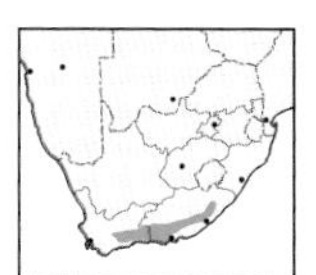

Cotyledon woodii

Wood's cotyledon

Plants are many-branched shrubs that may reach waist height and are well adorned with succulent, blue-green, rounded leaves, each of which has a pointed tip and a purple margin. Initially the stems are green, but they brown with age and the bark peels. During late summer, small inflorescences of one to three nodding flowers are presented on short inflorescence stalks just above the branches. These are orange to red, with lobes that spread back partially. This species prefers wooded ravines in valley bushveld, in which situations it can be locally abundant.

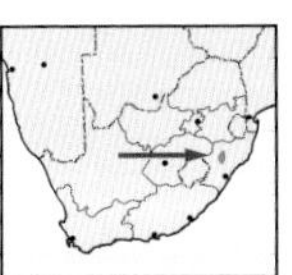

Crassula smithii

Plants usually grow in small, shrubby clumps consisting of a few, clustered, fairly open rosettes. Leaves are an unusual, light yellowish-green, covered with tiny red dots, and as thick as a man's little finger. The tips are tapered, but harmless. Flowers are bright crimson-red and carried in tight clusters that are borne erectly in summer. The range of this grassland species appears to be limited to central KwaZulu-Natal. The yellowish leaves and crimson flowers make this an attractive garden plant.

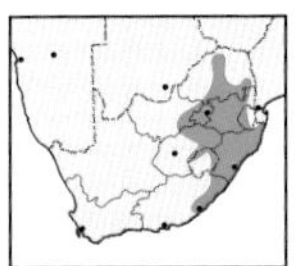

Crassula alba

Plants similar in appearance to *C. vaginata*, but when in flower the basal rosette tends to 'blow out', with larger leaves expanding along the flowering stem. The leaves are green, sometimes with purple markings, and are narrowly triangular to lance-shaped in outline. The inflorescences are not as flat-topped as those in *C. vaginata*, being more rounded, and ranging in colour from cream to deep red, sometimes even yellow. The flowers are fragrant, with

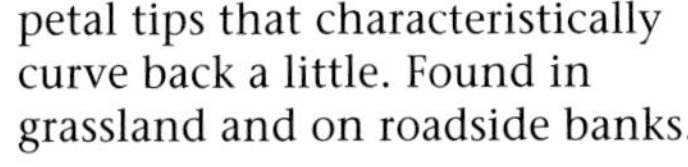

petal tips that characteristically curve back a little. Found in grassland and on roadside banks.

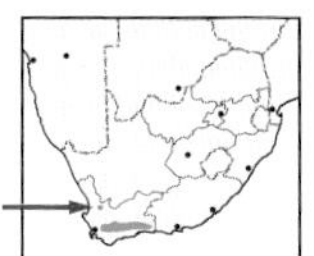

Crassula arborescens

Jade plant | *Boomplakkie*

Medium-sized shrubs to small trees that glow silvery as a result of their bluish-grey foliage. Leaves are round to slightly oval-shaped and have numerous small red dots on both surfaces, especially towards the margins. The divisions between finger-long stem sections tend to be constricted, as opposed to those of *C. ovata*, which are thickened. Flowers are white to light pink and carried in dense, ball-shaped clusters from early to mid-summer. The species occurs widely in southern and western South Africa, particularly in the Little Karoo.

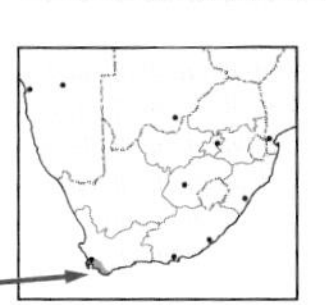

Crassula coccinea

Red crassula | *Klipblom*

Ankle- to knee-high shrublets that carry light green, roughly heart-shaped leaves clustered on several thin stems. The leaves have pointed, but harmless tips and are a pleasant light green. Radiant, crimson red flowers are borne in erect, umbrella-shaped clusters in mid- to late summer. This fynbos species grows well in gardens in winter-rainfall areas, but has to be replaced every few years as it dies or becomes scraggly after flowering.

Crassula columnaris subsp. *columnaris*

Khaki-button | *Koesnaatjie*

Plants grow as fat, miniature columns that carry their stems erectly. The stems are densely clothed in rounded leaves. In exposed positions the leaves turn light brown to army green, with tiny, darker coloured spots all over their surfaces. Flowers are creamy white and carried in tight clusters at the apex of the plants. After about a decade of growth they flower from mid-winter to early summer. The plants die after having flowered. Their natural habitat is arid karoo.

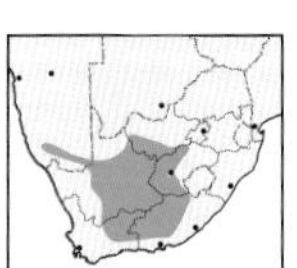

Crassula corallina

Coral crassula | *Hasiekos*

Small mats that grow to finger height at most, comprising a series of tightly packed stems covered with chunky, close-packed leaves. The blunt leaf tips are covered with a greyish wax layer, which gives the plant a delightful white-frosted look, especially obvious when the leaves spread a little to reveal their contrasting lime-green upper surfaces. The combination of slight wartiness, colour and form gives this species a coral-like appearance. The small, white flowers are produced singly from the stem tips during late summer. The tiny plants are often well camouflaged in their natural habitat, growing in full sun in shallow soil overlying rocks, sometimes with surface limestone.

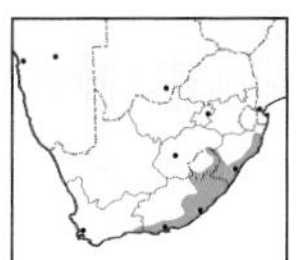

Crassula crenulata

Plants of this crassula are unusual in possessing swollen, underground tubers from which sparsely branched succulent stems arise. These reach about 50 cm in height, turning brown with age, although they are initially green with faint white dashes evident along their length. Leaves are produced in pairs, each stalkless and broadly lance-shaped. During late summer inflorescences of star-shaped, white flowers are produced at the top of the shoots. Such blooms may occasionally have a pink tinge. Its preferred habitat is on grassy slopes in the light shade of trees, where it is able to resprout from its tubers after fire.

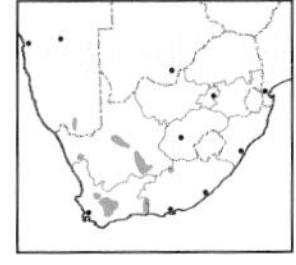

Crassula deltoidea

Small, knee-high shrublets with numerous radiating branches, giving them the appearance of miniature, ball-shaped trees. Leaves are deltoid to triangular, and a striking silvery white, with a tinge of pale pink and metallic blue. The whitish flowers are quite insignificant in comparison to the leaves, despite being carried in small, but dense bunches on elongated stalks. Even though it is a tough shrublet itself, the plant often tends to grow in the shade of other, non-succulent karoo shrubs.

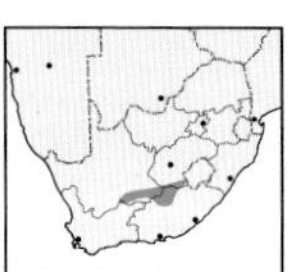

Crassula exilis subsp. *cooperi*

Plants of this low-growing species form dense cushions on the soil. Their leaf texture and colour are among the most attractive of the miniature crassulas. The numerous tiny rosettes of green to reddish-brown leaves have sunken dark spots on the upper surface. Quite stout hairs are present along the leaf margin. In bloom, plants reach only ankle height, the small white flowers appearing in late summer through early autumn. Found in the shade of overhanging rocks, or small patches of scrub.

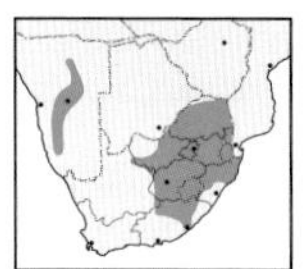

Crassula lanceolata subsp. *transvaalensis*

Plants rarely exceed 15 cm in height, being well branched from the base. The shoots are stiffly erect, with small, narrowly lance-shaped leaves paired along their length. Each leaf is sharp-tipped. Aerial plant portions die back over winter, to regenerate from the fleshy rootstock the following spring. During late summer the tiny, cup-shaped flowers are produced in tight clusters in the axils of the leaves. They are an inconspicuous yellowish-green, soon turning brown. Will tolerate some shading in the open bushveld and savanna in which it grows, usually in shallow soil pockets above rock. This subspecies extends northwards to central Africa.

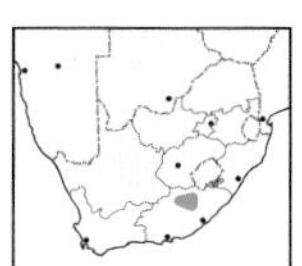

Crassula lanuginosa

Plants form mats with tight clusters of small, succulent leaves that are softly hairy, always with hairs along their margins. They are blue-green but turn red in high light conditions. A few white to cream, bell-shaped flowers are borne on a short inflorescence during late summer. These flowers bear stamens with black anthers. The plants are found along rock crevices and on rock sheets, often partly shaded by surrounding shrubs. They are sometimes found under overhanging rocks.

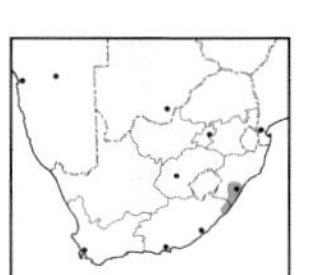

Crassula multicava subsp. *floribunda*

Specimens of subsp. *floribunda* form fleshy, few-branched shrubs to thigh height with stems as thick as a finger, covered with a light brown bark. Along their upperparts they bear either smooth or lightly hairy, egg-shaped leaves that are angled upwards. During mid-winter pure white flowers are produced in dense heads, each flower usually possessing five petals with recurved lobes. Plants are found in shaded ravines among rocks or on cliff edges, and are much less commonly encountered than subsp. *multicava*.

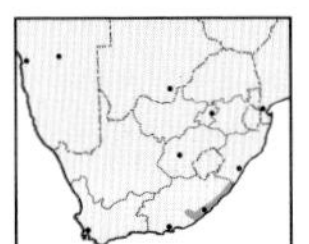

Crassula multicava subsp. *multicava*

Fairy crassula | *Skaduplakkie*

The leaves and all plant parts are hairless. The stems are green, flushed pink, and lean over, rooting from the nodes along their length. During winter they bear rounded inflorescences of pinkish-white flowers, each of which normally produces only four petals – a rare occurrence in the genus *Crassula*. Plants also produce plantlets (brood-buds) that bud directly off the inflorescence, particularly after flowering has completed. These result in rapid colony expansion, a feature that has contributed to the popularity of this succulent as a low-growing ground cover in horticulture. Plants grow in shaded areas among rocks, sometimes on cliff ledges along major estuaries.

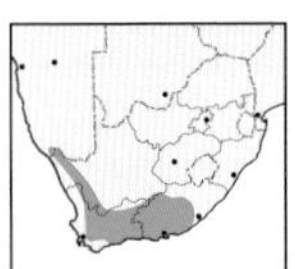

Crassula nemorosa

From small, perennial tubers, delicate blue-green stems are produced in spring, each usually shorter than finger length. The heart-shaped leaves are similarly glaucous and with an entire margin. Single, nodding cup-shaped flowers appear in winter, each petal being a silvery pink. The plants are tiny and barely noticeable, growing out of thin cracks on cliff faces with a cooler aspect, or otherwise between rocks on scree slopes.

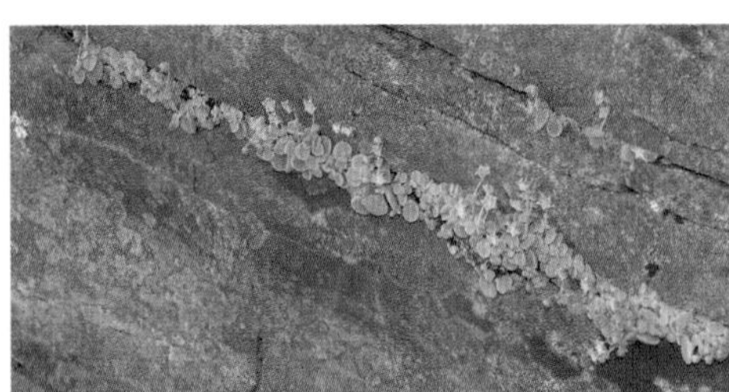

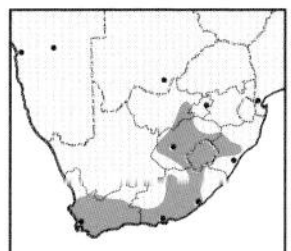

Crassula nudicaulis var. *nudicaulis*

This compact little leaf succulent has reddish-green leaves, sometimes with a maroon margin, which can also be lightly hairy. The rather insignificant and very small cream flowers are borne in clusters along the length of the inflorescence, or are bunched towards its tip. The flowering stem may reach 40 cm in height, though normally it is substantially shorter. This species is to be found on rock ledges and in crevices, usually in the partial shade of neighbouring shrubs.

Crassula orbicularis

Stone crassula | *Klipblom*

Plants occur as open rosettes about 10 cm across. The leaf margins are densely fringed with stiff, white hairs. The leaves are green, sometimes flushed pink when stressed, and with or without a purplish margin. Thin runners are sometimes produced, resulting in small plants cascading down the krantz sides below the colony. During the winter months (though sometimes into mid-summer) well-branched inflorescences are presented above the vegetative parts, each white flower resembling a tubular bell. Plants are always found sheltering in the shade, usually on rock ledges.

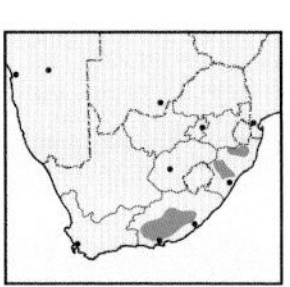

Crassula ovata

Money plant | *Beestebul*

Small to medium-sized shrubs or trees that resemble bonsai baobabs. Trunks are rough in texture, and a light brown to grey. The leaves are ovate and usually a bright, shiny green. Flowers are white, tinged with pink, very small and star-shaped. What the flowers lack in terms of size is made up for by the very dense, tennis ball-sized clusters in which they are carried. The species has a wide distribution range, from the southern Eastern Cape to KwaZulu-Natal.

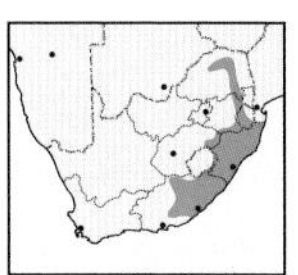

Crassula pellucida subsp. *brachypetala*

Given the diversity of its habitats, this species is highly variable in form: plants in grassveld often produce a small, succulent rhizome, while the leaves of plants in dry situations become purplish, particularly on their undersides, with purple spots above. The stems typically lie along the soil surface, growing to lengths of 60 cm, and rooting at their nodes. The leaves are egg- to broadly lance-shaped. During late summer and early autumn white- or pink-flushed, star-shaped flowers are borne in clusters at the tips of the well-branched stems. Plants are found in a variety of habitats from exposed grasslands to drip lines in partial shade, to the shade beneath dry bushveld vegetation. This species occurs northwards into tropical Africa.

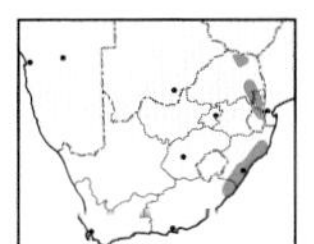

Crassula perfoliata var. *heterotricha*

Pointed-leaved crassula | *Heuningbossie*

The long, grey-green pointed leaves of this crassula are clustered at the ends of grey-brown stems. In larger cliff-dwelling plants, some pendulous stems may reach lengths of 30 cm, revealing their prominent internodes. Carries white, tubular flowers with five petal tips that curve backwards. Petals contrast strongly with the red styles and hairy red calyxes. Found in rocky grassland, and close to krantz edges, even growing on cliff ledges.

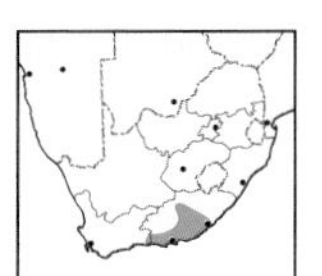

Crassula perfoliata var. *minor*

Scarlet paintbrush

The silvery grey leaves of this crassula are sickle-shaped and are vertically stacked at about right angles to each other. Leaves may have purple blotches. Plants are rarely branched, but reach shin height and produce a long-lasting, terminal inflorescence of open, bell-shaped flowers. These are usually scarlet, with pink to nearly white forms also known, and are produced in mid-summer. Occurs among rocky outcrops in grassland. The red-flowering form was a popular florist's flower in England during the Victorian era. Plants of this form are also known in horticulture as *C. perfoliata* var. *rubra*.

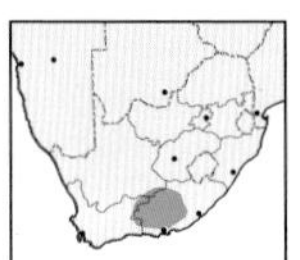

Crassula perfoliata var. *perfoliata*

Sosatie

Plants of this variety can grow to waist height, and may be sparsely branched. The boat-shaped leaves are held more or less erectly; they are blue-green in colour and have the outline of a lance, being broader at the base. Upright inflorescences are produced at the stem tips from late spring to mid-summer. The flowering shoots take the form of a silvery brown stem topped by a dense cluster of small, open white bells flushed pink in the centre. Their preferred habitat is in full sun among dry, karroid scrub on the lower slopes of hillsides.

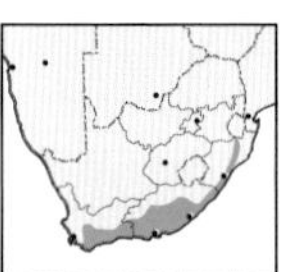

Crassula perforata

String-of-buttons

The thin, straggling stems of this species attain arm's length, but seldom branch. Their opposite, ovate leaves are fused to each other around the stem. Their arrangement gives the impression of a string of evenly spaced, square buttons. The leaves are blue-green and maroon towards their tips, and have horny margins coloured either yellow or red. During late summer tiny, creamy yellow flowers are borne on inflorescences that extend from the stem tips. Usually found on dry cliff faces or in rocky scrub.

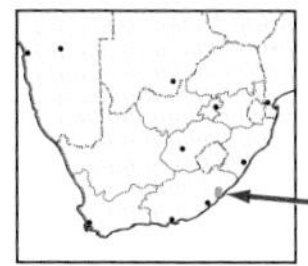

Crassula planifolia

Plants somewhat resemble *Crassula tetragona*, but are distinguishable by their much flatter leaves and winter- rather than summer- or autumn-flowering times. The slim, bonsai-like plants attain mid-shin height. Older stems are brown, sometimes with a flaky bark, while younger ones are green. Leaves are lance-shaped and dark green. Very small white flowers are borne in dense terminal inflorescences during mid-winter. *C. planifolia* may be found growing fully exposed in shallow rock pockets overlying rocky outcrops. Restricted to part of the Transkei region of the Eastern Cape.

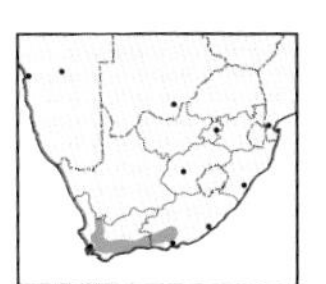

Crassula rupestris subsp. *rupestris*

Concertina plant | *Bergkraletjies*

Small, knee-high shrublets with branches that are quite thin and brittle. They have more-or-less egg-shaped, fat leaves that are a dull, bluish-green. The smooth, horny margins are usually broad and a sharply contrasting red to purple. The red leaf coloration is more intense in exposed positions. Flowers are white with a reddish tinge and carried in small clusters. Plants flower from mid-winter to spring. The species occurs in a broad band from near Cape Town in the west to north of Port Elizabeth in the east, through the Little Karoo.

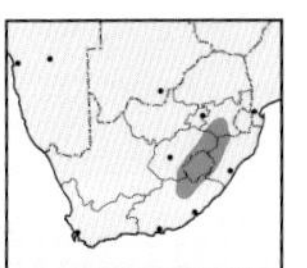

Crassula sarcocaulis subsp. *rupicola*

Plants are bonsai-like, with short, thickened stems and basal branches, at first upright and then leaning, so giving plants a windswept appearance. The branches, with their reddish-brown peeling bark, bear blue-grey leaves mostly towards the stem tips. These leaves are broadest nearest their base. During late summer and early autumn red buds appear in dense inflorescences that cover the knee-high plants. These open to reveal a spectacular display of light pink or white flowers. Plants are usually found on cooler slopes, tucked in at the base of protective boulders at higher altitude.

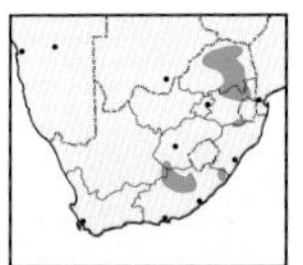

Crassula sarcocaulis subsp. *sarcocaulis*

Plants grow as smooth-stemmed shrubs with small, bright green, shield-shaped leaves densely carried in diminutive, tree-like canopies. In winter, plants are more or less leafless, especially in cold areas, exposing the grey stems that give the plants their miniature baobab-like appearance. Small, white flowers are borne in clusters in autumn and early winter, just before the temperatures drop too low. This savanna species from the mild temperate eastern parts of South Africa is gaining in popularity among gardeners, given that it is very easy to grow in open beds or in containers, even tiny ones.

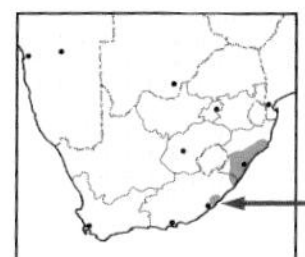

Crassula sarmentosa

The long, slender running stems of this species set it apart from most other crassulas. The dark green leaves have a finely serrate margin, on the inside of which a row of gland dots is evident. The white flowers have a hint of pink in them, especially when in bud, and are arranged in rounded inflorescences with each flower set at about 90 degrees to its neighbour. With its scandent stems this species clambers over neighbouring shrubs and grass clumps on rocky outcrops and at the margins of the bushveld vegetation that it inhabits.

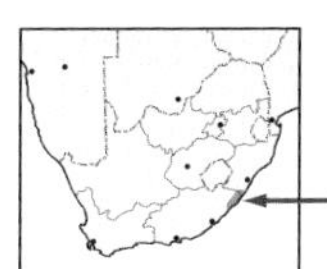

Crassula streyi

Pondoland crassula

Plants are compact, reclining herbs. The large, oval leaves have distinctive purplish-red undersides, and dark green upper surfaces that appear variegated on account of the contrasting light green veins. The leaves are compressed into a basal rosette, with successive leaf pairs arranged at right angles to each other. The leaf margins curve downwards. In more exposed situations such as on estuarine cliffs, *C. streyi* sometimes grows alongside the more vigorous *C. multicava* subsp. *multicava* with which it can be confused at first glance. The white flowers are borne on inflorescences 15 cm tall. This handsome crassula is a specialist of shady rock ledges and moist forest earthbanks, always close to watercourses. Its range is limited to the coastal region of northern Pondoland and southern KwaZulu-Natal.

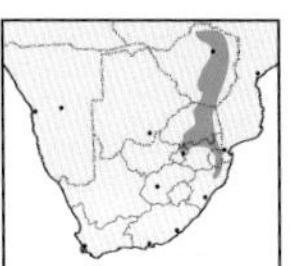

Crassula swaziensis

Low-growing, multi-branched shrublets that carry fat, succulent leaves in the upper halves of the branches. The branches are thin, fairly brittle and appear old, even when still young. Leaves are ovate to broadly sickle-shaped and softly furry. Leaf colour is somewhat variable, depending on where the plants grow: they are greener in the shade, and brownish in exposed situations. Small white flowers that are pink in the bud stage are borne in tight clusters, carried on elongated stalks. The species flowers from autumn to late winter. It has a wide distribution range in the northern part of central South Africa, particularly in grasslands and savannas.

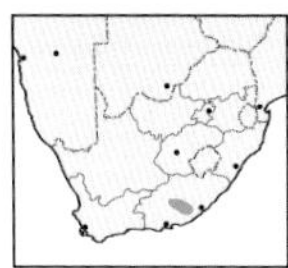

Crassula tetragona subsp. *robusta*

Karkai

Robust shrubs up to 1 m tall. The stems and branches of this crassula are much thicker and stronger than those of the other subspecies in *C. tetragona*. The stems are erect and branch moderately, each branch orientating itself vertically. The pointed leaves are shaped like miniature samurai swords. They are arranged in crossed pairs along the upper portions of the brown stems. Accordingly, if viewed from above, they are arranged in four distinct vertical rows. Both leaves and stems are hairless. The quite insignificant bell-shaped flowers, borne in mid- to late summer, are creamy white, soon turning brown. They are carried in small clusters at the tips of branches. This Eastern Cape species is found in the partial shade of karroid scrub.

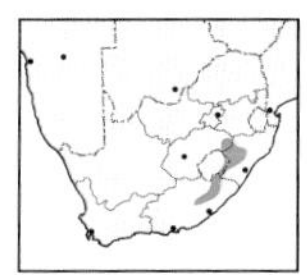

Crassula umbraticola

This diminutive species has a delicate, upright stem, just a few centimetres high and bears short-stalked, rounded leaves with shallowly lobed margins. The tiny, creamy white flowers – borne during late summer – are presented in open, branched inflorescences above the plants. This species is shade-loving, found in cool, moist forests beneath overhanging rocks or in damp caves. It may be found growing embedded in moss along the length of drip lines. Most likely to be encountered in the KwaZulu-Natal Drakensberg, the region to which it is largely restricted.

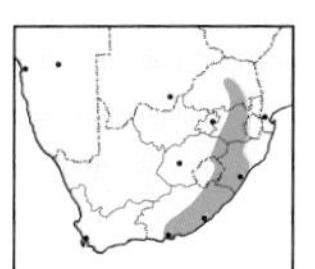

Crassula vaginata

Yellow or white crassula

The stem base is attached to a tuber from which the narrowly triangular leaf pairs emerge. They are arranged spirally in a rosette, with the largest leaves found lower down. Higher up the stem, the bases of leaves opposite one another fuse to form a characteristic sheath around the stem. In bloom, individuals can reach knee-height, with a mass of tightly packed yellow or white flowers presented at the stem apex. These flat-topped inflorescences are somewhat cauliflower-like in appearance. Plants occur in open, moist grassland.

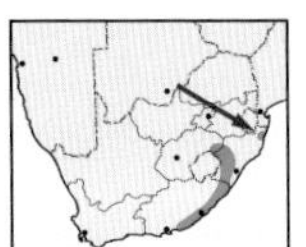

Kalanchoe crenata

Orange forest kalanchoe | *Plakkie*

An upright, multi-stemmed herb. The dark green, succulent leaves have irregularly shaped margins with blunt teeth, and petioles with wings along their length. Inflorescences are produced during late autumn and winter, reaching thigh height and presenting rounded heads of long, tubular orange flowers. Each flower is topped with four flared lobes and clasped by a light green calyx. After flowering, all aerial parts die back to a persistent rootstock, having expended their energies in the production of copious dust-like seed. Few kalanchoes thrive in moist, shady situations but this is one species that does just that: it prefers the undergrowth at the margins of mist-belt forests, growing on both earth banks and mossy rocks. Although rarely encountered, *K. crenata* may be locally abundant, its bright orange blooms obvious in the dim light of its forest abode.

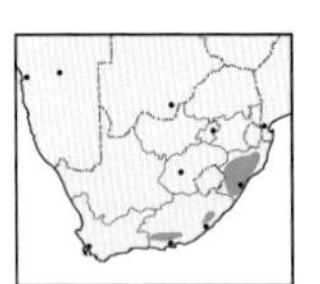

Kalanchoe hirta

Yellow hairy kalanchoe | *Plakkie*

Both stems and leaves are succulent and hairy, with leaf margins often coarsely toothed, and the leaves themselves folding inwards. Its flowers are yellow to light orange, and are produced in winter in terminal inflorescences that reach knee height. After fruiting, the flowering shoot dies back to a succulent rootstock with several persistent, low-growing shoots. This hairy species has in the past been confused with *K. crenata*, but is found growing in much drier situations, in valley bushveld, or on exposed rock ledges in open grasslands.

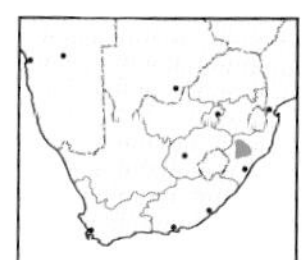

Kalanchoe longiflora

Plants are low-growing to creeping leaf succulents with stems that are thin, fairly brittle and angled. The round leaves have wavy indentations along their margins and are sea green, tinged with orange. Inflorescences are borne in autumn to mid-winter, well branched, fairly dainty and carry numerous tubular, yellow flowers. Since stems tend to be unable to remain erect as a result of the weight of the fat, albeit flattened, leaves, these plants make an excellent ground cover in sunny or dappled shady positions. The species is restricted to the central Tugela River basin of KwaZulu-Natal.

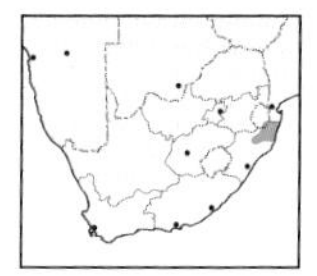

Kalanchoe neglecta

Plants reach about knee height and resemble *K. rotundifolia* in several respects. They are distinguished from that species by the presence of heart-shaped bases to the leaves, and leaves that often fold upwards, especially when drought stressed. The leaf margins are scalloped. The plants bear short, tubular, yellow to orange flowers in a terminal inflorescence. May be found growing in the sandy soils of the coastal plains of Maputaland, or up in the Lebombo Mountains, in semi-shade on rock ledges and cliff faces along the dry river valleys.

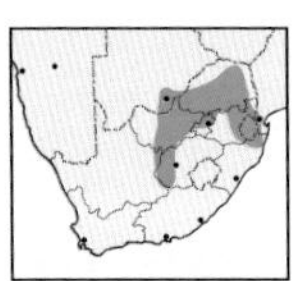

Kalanchoe paniculata

Large orange kalanchoe | *Hasiesoor*

Low-growing to loosely shrubby leaf succulents. The stems tend to become top-heavy and easily topple over. Leaves are oval-shaped and a light green colour. In mid-winter a tall, well-branched, open inflorescence is produced at the tip of a branch. Flowers are quite small, tubular and a bright, greenish-yellow. Small plants sprout from the base after the plant has flowered. The species has a wide distribution range in eastern southern Africa, but does not enter the more climatically severe Karoo.

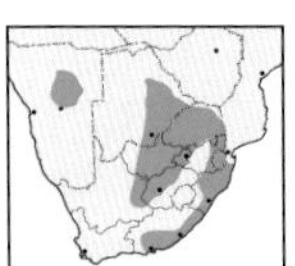

Kalanchoe rotundifolia

Common kalanchoe | *Nentabos, plakkie*

Sparsely branched, erect plants, usually with blue-green leaves that may or may not have a stalk. The leaves are generally egg-shaped, but this may vary considerably along with the colour and the character of their margins, which may be rounded, toothed or lobed. That considerably different variants can be found growing alongside each other suggests that more than one species is in fact involved. Between autumn and mid-summer orange to scarlet four-lobed flowers are produced in inflorescences borne high above the vegetative parts, with about one-third of the flowers open at any one time. Both before and after flowering the floral lobes tend to twist about themselves. Found growing in groups in the semi-shade of open woodland or thicket. Plants are extremely common in the northern parts of southern Africa and are among the most likely succulents to be encountered. Their range extends far northwards into East Africa and even to the island of Socotra.

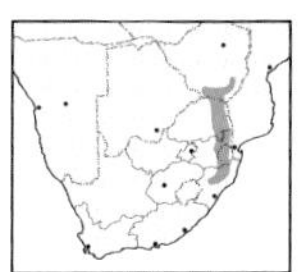

Kalanchoe sexangulares

Low-growing shrublets, with fairly thin, angled stems that carry large, heart-shaped leaves on prominent stalks. Leaves have conspicuous marginal indentations. Especially in exposed positions the leaves turn a bright crimson red. From August to November small, yellow flowers are borne on tall, open inflorescences. Plants grow exceedingly easily and will produce a bright red carpet if grown *en masse* in areas that receive a lot of direct sunlight. The species occurs widely in the northern and eastern parts of South Africa, especially in savanna vegetation.

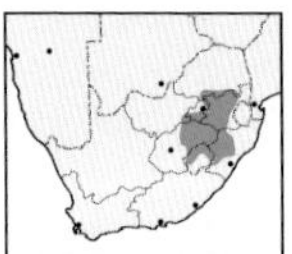

Kalanchoe thyrsiflora

White lady | *Geelplakkie*

Plants are low-growing, usually unbranched leaf succulents. Leaf scars appear low down on the very short, grey-blue stem, where leaves have become detached. Some forms of the species are more prone to sucker from the base, giving rise to small clumps of plants. Leaves are borne erectly and are the size and shape of soup plates. They are blue-grey for the most part, as a result of a thick powdery bloom, but tend to become red-tinged towards the margin. After about two years, plants produce a tall inflorescence carrying small, creamy-yellow, densely arranged flowers. The species flowers in mid-winter. It occurs very widely in South Africa's grasslands and savannas.

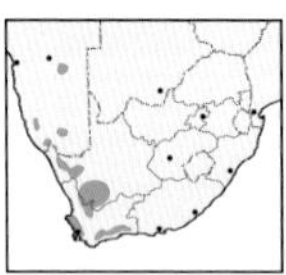

Tylecodon paniculatus

Butter tree | *Botterboom*

Small to medium-sized, chunky trees. The stems are very fat, mustard yellow to light greenish in colour, and shed flaky bark in peeling strips. Leaves are thickly succulent, oval-shaped and a verdant light green. Plants are deciduous and shed their leaves in winter. Inflorescence stalks are an attractive, bright crimson red and carry rather insignificant yellowish, tubular flowers. The species occurs commonly in the arid, mostly winter-rainfall regions of southern and western South Africa.

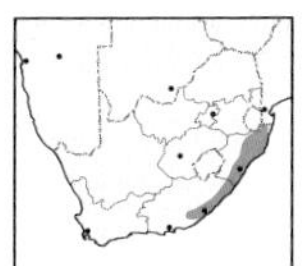

Gerrardanthus macrorhizus

This remarkable succulent bears a silver-brown pumpkin-like caudex, usually about 40 cm in diameter. A long trailing shoot is produced from the upper surface; this branches and, with the aid of branched tendrils, climbs neighbouring shrubs and trees to a height of 8 m. The smooth, alternate leaves are ivy-shaped (three- to seven-lobed), shiny (particularly on their undersides) and prominently veined. Unlike its close relative *G. tomentosus*, the leaves and stems are without a covering of downy hairs. Small, glossy brown flowers grow from the leaf axils, male and female flowers being produced on separate plants. The pendulous fruit, which resembles a sea cucumber, opens at the lower tip to release a number of large, papery, winged seeds. Found on rocky ledges in valley bushveld regions on the east coast.

Gerrardanthus tomentosus

Plants possess large, pumpkin-like caudices that can attain a diameter of over 1 m. From the edge of the upper surface of this greyish-brown caudex, one or more long shoots emerge. These trail for a short distance before climbing up to 15 m into the surrounding vegetation to rise to the light above, or trail to the bright forest margin. The deep green, five- to seven-lobed leaves are downy below, particularly along the prominent veins. All young plant parts are also downy. Male and female flowers are borne on separate plants during late summer, the small and shiny brown blooms being quite inconspicuous. The fruits are dry, 10-ribbed pods that hang downwards to release their winged seeds to the wind. The enormous caudices lie exposed on rock ledges, appearing boulder-like on the forest floor.

Dioscorea elephantipes

Elephant's foot | *Olifantsvoet*

The grey, fleshy caudex of this species can reach a height of 1 m with age. These columnar, stem-like structures are mostly above ground and become deeply and quite regularly incised to form six- to seven-angled knobs that resemble corky warts. From the caudex top a multitude of much-branched wiry shoots emerge; each bears kidney-shaped or nearly three-lobed leaves. Sprays of yellow-green flowers are produced during late summer and autumn, with male and female flowers borne by separate plants. The seeds are broadly winged. This is a species of rocky hillsides in the drier regions of South Africa. Plant numbers were reduced substantially during the 1950s when many tons of plants were harvested and extracted locally for the international pharmaceutical industry.

Dioscorea sylvatica

Forest elephant's foot
Skilpadknol

The fleshy caudex is often situated below ground but may also be seen at the soil surface when growing in the humus of shallow soil pockets. The caudex surface texture is less incised than that of *D. elephantipes*, and is patterned like a tortoise shell. The caudex is often irregularly lobed, and flattened to a low dome shape. One or two wiry, aerial shoots emerge from a growing point at the top of this organ, to climb high into the canopy above; these bear heart-shaped, leathery leaves with a sharp tip. The yellow-green flowers are produced in summer on separate male and female plants. Occurs mostly in forests both along the coast and inland in the mist-belt region, although they occur also in drier regions such as the Lebombos. As with *D. elephantipes*, this species was historically harvested as a source of diosgenin to produce contraceptives and cortisone.

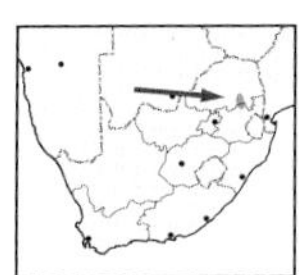

Dracaena transvaalensis

Wolkberg dragon-tree
Wolkberg-drakeboom

Small, mostly single-trunked trees, although some mature specimens do branch extensively. The trunks are straight and leafless for most of their length, with stiff, greyish-green leaves that are quite long and borne horizontally or erectly, especially when they are still young. Leaves are ribbed below and distinctly succulent, especially towards their bases. When particularly drought stressed, leaves roll under along their length. Flowers are small, white and carried in large clusters. They are followed by reddish-orange berries. The species has a restricted distribution range in northern South Africa where it grows exposed on dry, rocky hillsides.

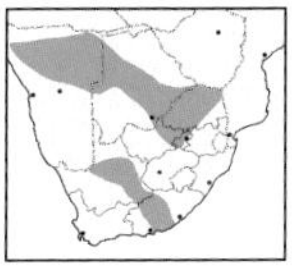

Sansevieria aethiopica

Bowstring hemp | *Wildewortel*

Plants grow as shin- to knee-high tufts that consist of a few recurved, half-folded leaves arising straight from the ground. Leaves are slightly rough to the touch, and mottled with cross-banded, alternating light green and darker green sections. In mid-summer, the short inflorescences carry white to purple, slightly fragrant flowers. The flowers are quite large for such small plants and appear even larger as a result of the strongly recurved flower tips. Fertilised flowers are replaced by decorative, marble-sized, orange fruit. The species has a wide distribution in South Africa's more arid grasslands, and beyond into Botswana and Namibia.

Sansevieria hyacinthoides

Mother-in-law's tongue | *Skoonma-se-tong*

Grows in erect tufts that consist of a few short to medium-length, sword-shaped leaves rising straight from the ground. Leaves are a light, dull green or mottled with light green spots against a drab background. In mid-summer, short inflorescences carry white, slightly fragrant flowers. As with *S. aethiopica*, flowers appear disproportionately large, have strongly recurved flower tips and are followed by small orange fruit. The species has a wide distribution in South Africa's woodlands and rocky outcrops, and beyond.

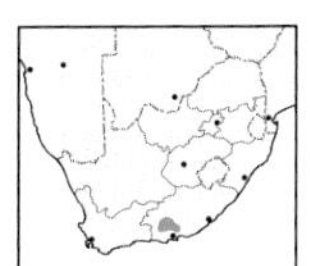

Euphorbia caerulescens

Noorsdoring

These medium-sized shrubs consist of numerous, erect branches that curve gracefully upwards. Branches arise from a single, short stem near ground level and are segmented into little sections. Small yellow inflorescences are carried along the stem angles. If the stems are chopped into finger-length segments and left to dry for a few days, sheep and goats will pick them up as a substitute for fodder. The species is exceedingly common in the arid eastern Karoo; the *noorsveld* is named after it.

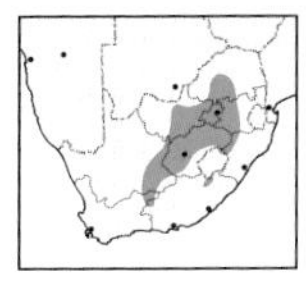

Euphorbia clavarioides var. *truncata*

Lion's spoor | *Vingerpol*

Plants resemble large, round scatter cushions sunk halfway into the ground. They consist of small, densely clustered, erect branchlets on a short, but prominent, horizontally flattened stem. The branchlets are dull green, somewhat warty and carry short-lived, ellipse-shaped leaves. Small, dirty-yellow pseudo-flowers are carried from autumn to spring. The species is a typical element of South Africa's once vast grasslands.

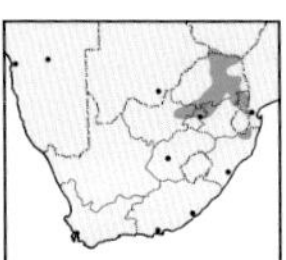

Euphorbia cooperi var. *cooperi*

Deadliest euphorbia | *Noorsdoring*

These massive, single-trunked trees consist of numerous branches that tend to bend downwards before turning skywards. The branches are bright green and distinctly angled. Branches are also divided into inverted teardrop-shaped segments that carry short, very sharp spines. In mid-winter bright yellow inflorescences that resemble small flowers are carried on the stem segment margins. This savanna tree is scattered through much of northern South Africa.

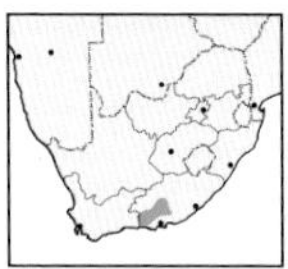

Euphorbia enopla var. *enopla*

These small to knee-high shrublets carry numerous, finger-thick stems in erect to spreading clusters. The stems are leafless, bright green and adorned with contrasting red to purple spines. These radiate horizontally from the stems. The spines are, in fact, the persistent remains of the short inflorescence stalks. Small, yellowish pseudo-flowers are carried during summer. The species is more or less restricted to the Little and Great Karoo of South Africa.

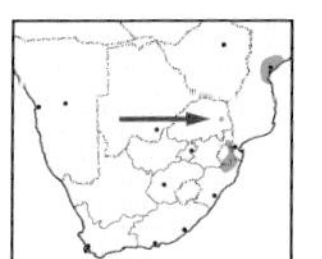

Euphorbia grandicornis subsp. *grandicornis*

Big thorn euphorbia | *Grootdoringnaboom*

Plants grow as large, robust shrubs to small trees that have several thick branches arising from a short, central, underground stem. The branches are angled, regularly constricted into thick sections, and gracefully curve upwards and outwards. Branch margins carry rows of quite long, forked, decorative but menacing spines. The flattened sides of the branches are sometimes beautifully mottled with lighter green to yellowish-green skeleton-like patterns. White milky latex exudes where the stem is damaged. From early winter to spring, small yellow pseudo-flowers are produced on the upperparts of the branches, followed by fat, reddish fruit. The species is widespread in the savannas and thickets of eastern South Africa (northern KwaZulu-Natal, Mpumalanga), Swaziland and Mozambique, and further north into Tanzania and Kenya.

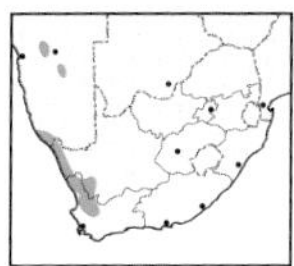

Euphorbia hamata

Olifantsmelkbos

Plants are low growing and scraggly, with a multitude of thin, floppy branches extending from a central point outwards. Branches are covered with short, blunt projections. The small leaves are short-lived. Inflorescences, the small pseudo-flowers, have prominent, distinctly greenish bracts that are tinged with red, and are borne from April to September. The species prefers the winter-rainfall, arid part of western southern Africa as its natural habitat.

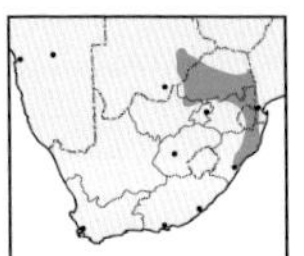

Euphorbia ingens

Naboom euphorbia | *Naboom*

Plants are also sometimes referred to as *E. candelabrum* and form medium-sized to very large trees. The numerous, erect branches curve upwards, so that the canopy resembles an oversized egg cup. The greyish trunks are unbranched low down, and have a rough texture. They tend to lean to one side so that the canopies seem too heavy to be supported. Branches are light green, prominently angled, and carry short, sharp spines along the margins. Where damaged, the plants bleed white, milky latex that is sure to irritate exposed skin. Leaves are absent. The diminutive yellow pseudo-flowers, which appear from April to July, exude copious amounts of nectar. These trees are widely dispersed in the northern savannas of southern Africa. A town, Naboomspruit in the Limpopo province of South Africa, was named for this conspicuous species.

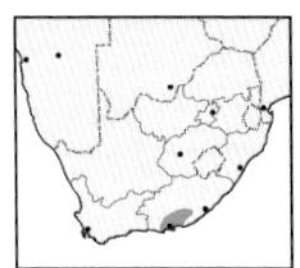

Euphorbia ledienii var. *ledienii*

Suurnoors

Plants are robust deciduous shrubs with erect stems that sometimes topple over. The fleshy stems are angled and carry small, sharp spines along their margins. When broken, plants bleed a milky white latex. The pseudo-flowers are bright yellow, and carried near the tips of the stems from mid-winter to spring. The flowers, and ultimately the fruit, give the stems a distinct baseball-bat shape as they tend to thicken the upperparts of the stems. The species is common in the thickets of the Eastern Cape.

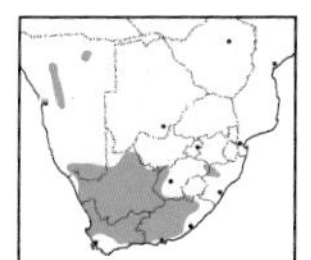

Euphorbia mauritanica

Milk bush | *Geelmelkbos*

These deciduous shrublets carry small, narrow, short-lived leaves clustered on the new growth of branches. The branches are fleshy and cylindrical, and rapidly exude white, milky latex where damaged. The pseudo-flowers are bright yellow, and carried near the tips of the stems from mid-winter to spring. This is one of the most common pencil-stemmed euphorbias that occurs in South Africa. It has an exceedingly wide distribution range through the arid regions of southern Africa.

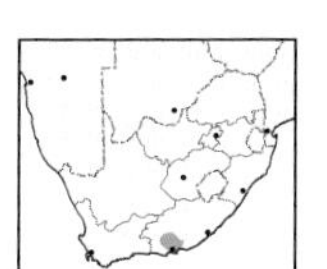

Euphorbia meloformis

Skilpadkos

Small, dome-shaped and leafless, these succulents remain unbranched, hugging the soil closely. However, as with many succulents, plants will clump with age, creating a cluster of plant bodies that somewhat resembles the roof of the Kremlin. The stems are light green, ribbed and cross-banded with reddish lines. The rib margins carry short inflorescence stalks. From early summer to autumn the plants carry minuscule yellowish-green pseudo-flowers. Male and female are on separate plants. Small depressions are left where the inflorescence stalks are ultimately shed. The species is restricted to the Eastern Cape.

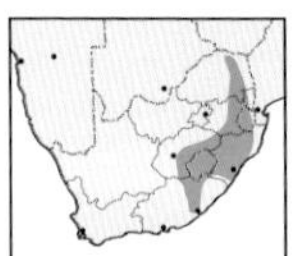

Euphorbia pulvinata

Prickly-leaved cushion euphorbia | *Voetangel*

A highly variable, mound-forming species comprised of tightly packed, seven- to ten-angled green stems. At its apex, each succulent stem bears a straight, grey thorn on each angled lobe and small, barely noticeable leaves that soon become deciduous. The cushion-like mounds are sometimes rounded and at other times irregularly lobed, with very old plants attaining a height of 1.5 m. From spring through to mid-summer small yellow to red-brown flowers are produced at the branch tips. Other succulents can often be found growing on the mounds of this cold-tolerant species. Grows exposed in rocky grassland, or on rock sheets.

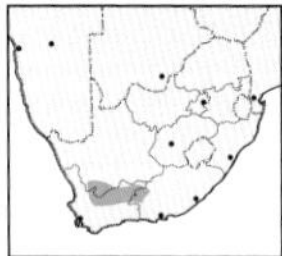

Euphorbia stellispina

Grootnoors

A succulent shrub with columnar to club-shaped stems that branch to form small, cactus-like clusters. The stems carry spines in the middle and lower down, while the upperparts are devoid of spines, until the next season's flowering occurs. The spines are star-shaped at their tips, arranged in distinctive, vertical rows. These decorative spines are actually persistent inflorescence stalks. The pseudo-flowers are yellow, while the young inflorescence stalks are light purple, drying to a greyish-brown. Found in the arid Karoo regions of South Africa.

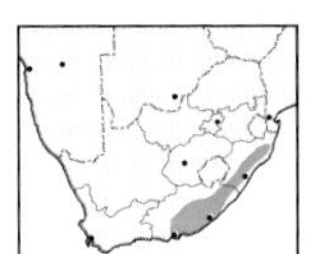

Euphorbia tetragona

Honey euphorbia | *Bosnaboom, Riviernaboom*

Robust trees that consist of a central stem from which numerous branches radiate. Branches tend to curve gracefully out- and upwards from the stem. With age, the branches are shed, often leaving a short section attached to the stem. The branches are four- to six-angled, and carry short, very sharp spines on their margins. When young, the stem and branches are light green but turn a light greyish-brown with age. The small, egg-shaped leaves are soon shed. Inflorescences are borne from June to August. They are bright yellow and consist of both male and female reproductive organs. These trees typically occur in valleys of the Eastern Cape, northwards to KwaZulu-Natal, where they often grow densely clustered in impenetrable thicket vegetation.

Euphorbia tirucalli

Rubber euphorbia
Kraalnaboom

A succulent tree species, reaching 12 m in height, though normally about 7 m, spreading to develop a rounded crown. The main stems are straight and rounded, with rough, grey bark. The cylindrical branchlets are highly divided and angled upwards. Though without spines, plants yield toxic, sticky latex when broken. While branchlets are normally green, attractive bronze-coloured branches (chimaeras) may occasionally be encountered in the veld. These have high horticultural appeal, and may be grown from cuttings. Plants are found in valley bushveld, on rocky outcrops and dry krantz edges.

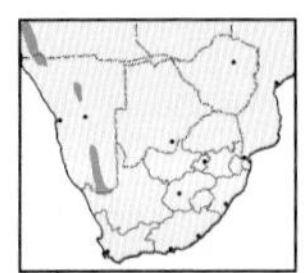

Euphorbia virosa subsp. *virosa*

Gifbos

Plants grow as erect, bushy shrubs that consist of several thickened, bright green branches sprouting from near ground level to a height of over 2 m. The branches are conspicuously angled and constricted into short, thick sections. Short, stout, greyish spines are neatly arranged along the branch margins. The tiny, flower-shaped inflorescences are bright yellow and borne in summer. The species occurs in the arid western coastal areas of southern Africa, through Namibia and into Angola.

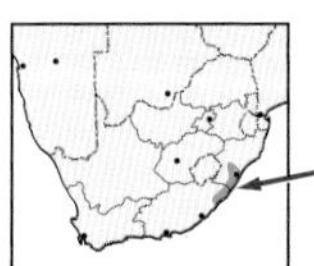

Euphorbia woodii

Wood's euphorbia | *Vingerpol*

Plants of this dwarf succulent may reach a diameter of up to 50 cm, although they are usually narrower. These have a central stem, most of which is buried. From this stem, a series of finger-thick branches radiate outwards. These are spineless, with tiny green-purple leaves set at right angles. The overall effect is of a medusa-like head growing prostrate on the soil surface. Flowering occurs throughout the year, the small bright yellow pseudo-flowers clustering in the centre of the plant. Plants are rather inconspicuous in their grassland habitat and usually occur within 30 km of the coast, where they clearly benefit from the humidity.

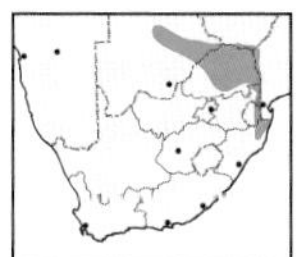

Monadenium lugardiae

Monadenium

A shrub with several erect and closely clustered succulent stems that reach knee height. Older stem sections are smooth and silvery brown while younger sections are green, with a quilted appearance. The spoon-shaped fleshy leaves are clustered towards the stem apices, as are the flowers, which appear from spring to mid-summer. Male and female flowers are produced within cup-like bracts, and borne on separate plants. The leaves are normally winter deciduous. Plants are found in partial shade in dry, rocky areas of the lowveld.

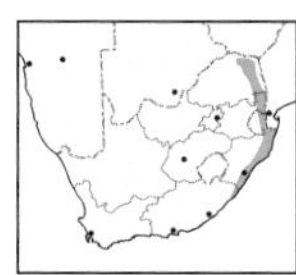

Synadenium cupulare

Dead-man's tree
Dooiemansboom

A shrub or small tree of up to 5 m. With its silvery main stem and branches, conspicuous leaf scars, and simple leaves clustered towards the branch ends, one could initially confuse this species with the exotic frangipani. The shiny leaves are succulent, dark green above and lighter below, with purple veins. Some variants bear leaves with prominently purple-flecked undersides, and purple spots above. The euphorbia-like flowers are produced in branched heads during late summer and autumn. All plant parts yield very toxic white latex. Found within, or on the margin of, bush clumps in rocky terrain such as granite outcrops.

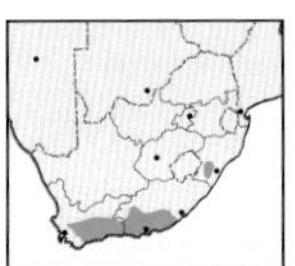

Pelargonium peltatum

Ivy-leaved pelargonium | *Kolsuring*

Creeping scramblers that, in time, form large sweeps of tangled stems that rest on surrounding plants. The stems are quite thin and brittle, and support heart- to kidney-shaped leaves that are flattened, but thickened with accumulated water, and have a softly shining appearance. In addition, the leaves of several forms of the species bear a crescent-shaped reddish to light purplish zone on their upper surfaces. Flowers vary from pale pink to purple, and are borne from spring to mid-summer. The species occurs over much of the southern parts of the Western and Eastern Cape. This is one of the species used in Europe to develop the so-called ivy-leaved geranium hybrids that are widely grown as balcony and windowsill plants.

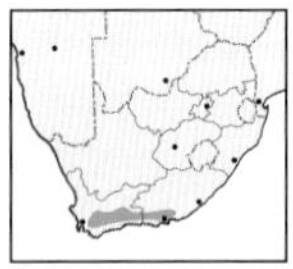

Pelargonium tetragonum

Square-stemmed pelargonium

These scraggly shrubs consist of a tangled mass of stems carrying very few leaves. The stems are three- to four-angled and dull green. Leaves are kidney- to heart-shaped and vary from smooth to hairy. Flowers are either creamy white or light pink, in both instances with prominent reddish, longitudinal streaks. Plants flower from spring to mid-summer, and occur in a broad band from the Worcester area, through the Little Karoo to Grahamstown in the Eastern Cape.

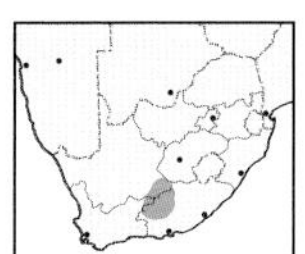

Sarcocaulon camdeboense

Candle bush | *Kersbos*

This species is also referred to as *Monsonia camdeboensis*. Plants are low-growing shrubs (to 30 cm), and are usually broader than they are high. Most branches grow roughly parallel to the ground. The stems have waxy, greyish-orange bark and long grey spines. The small, succulent leaves are deciduous during winter, when plants are exposed to severe frost. When present, the leaves are folded upwards slightly, and have an entire purplish margin. The pale yellow, open-faced flowers appear during mid-summer. Plants are typically found in the Karoo, in shallow soil pockets overlying rock, particularly dolerite or shale. They grow in full sun.

Scaevola plumierii

Beach plakkie
Strandplakkie

Plants are typically scramblers on coastal sand dunes. Stems are fairly thin and short and carry large, round to oblong, widely spaced, succulent leaves. Flowers are small, white and quite inconspicuous. This is one succulent that is probably not grown at all by collectors. Still, it is very widely encountered, virtually along the entire southern and eastern coastline of South Africa and beyond towards eastern tropical Africa. The leaves of this species seem immune to the harsh wind storms, salt spray and heat encountered along exposed beach dunes.

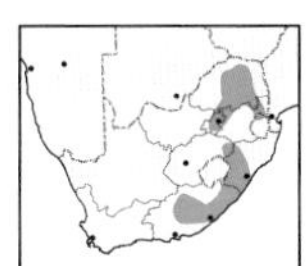

Bowiea volubilis

Climbing lily | *Knolklimop*

Plants of this strangely leafless bulb species produce a well-branched, climbing inflorescence. This clambers a short distance over and between nearby shrubs. The succulent green inflorescence has taken over the function of photosynthesis. The large, flattened bulbs are comprised of succulent, chunky scales and may sometimes be partly exposed at the soil surface. Yellow-green flowers appear during spring and summer, followed by green capsules that dry and turn brown before releasing their flattened black seeds. Most likely to be found on rocky outcrops or betweeen boulders on forest margins.

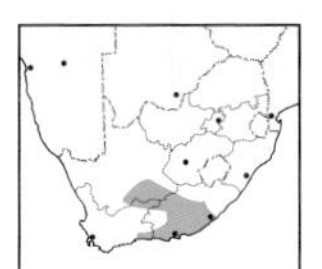

Ledebouria socialis

Plants grow as tightly packed clusters of small bulbs on the surface of the soil, each with several lance-shaped leaves. The plants normally take one of two forms: bulbs may be purple, with emergent leaves that have purple undersides and are silvery with green spots above; alternatively, the bulbs are green, and the leaves green below and silvery above, with green spots. In some instances the leaves are uniformly green. During early to mid-summer the pink and dull green bell-shaped flowers are presented on short, erect inflorescences. Colonies of this species are restricted to the Eastern Cape, where they may be found in the shade of plants in valley bushveld.

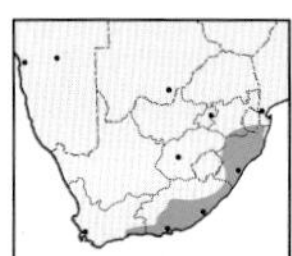

Ornithogalum longibracteatum

Pregnant onion | *Jeukbol*

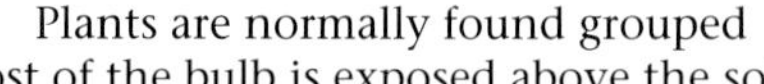

Plants are normally found grouped in clumps. Most of the bulb is exposed above the soil surface, the outer bulb scale (tunic) being dry and silvery brown. Bursting through this thin tunic are small bulbils, which eventually fall off to root at the base of the parent. Long, light green and recurved leaves are produced for most of the year, between which very tall and upright inflorescences appear during summer. These bear several hundred whitish-green flowers that, in bud, are accompanied by very long bracts. Occurs in a variety of habitats – fully exposed on rock sheets, or within forests between rocks.

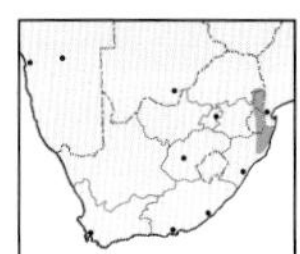

Urginea epigea

Tall white squill | *Jeukbol*

Plants grow as small clumps of bulbs. These bulbs are almost entirely exposed above the soil surface, and are an attractive silver-grey, with each chunky bulb scale in part overlapping the one above. Plants are winter deciduous, producing new, erect blue-green leaves immediately after flowering in spring. At this time tall inflorescences emerge, densely covered with small white flowers, each with recurved tepals bearing a central greenish-brown stripe. Occurs in hot lowveld regions. Outside of its natural range this species is reluctant to flower in cultivation.

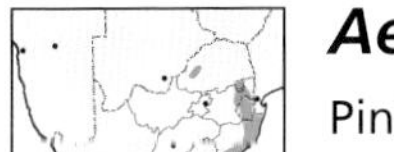

Aeollanthus parvifolius

Pink spur bush

Knee-high shrubs, with swollen bases to their greyish-brown stems. Often straggly-looking. The small, thickly succulent leaves are roundish in outline, smooth and blue green. They bear short leaf stalks and are clustered on short branches. The flowers are produced during summer and autumn on well-branched inflorescences. The white to light mauve flowers have purple spots on their upper lip. When found, they are always on rock sheets or krantz edges, exposed to bright light.

Plectranthus amboinicus

Indian mint, Country borage | *Kruie-spoorsalie*

Herbs with many stems that trail along rocky slopes. The leaves are crisply succulent and highly variable in size, and all forms bear a pleasant, sage-like scent. All plant parts, including the flowers, are lightly hairy. The flowers are white to lilac and borne on slender, spike-like, ascending inflorescences. This species occurs in drier areas, often in river valleys, from inland of Durban northwards into Kenya, and is believed to have been taken to India by early voyagers, hence the common name Indian mint. It is used to flavour food.

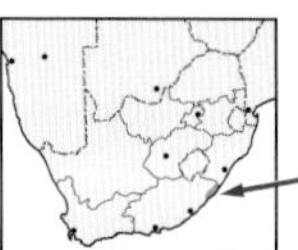

Plectranthus ernstii

Bonsai mint

Plants reach only 20 cm in height. The bases of the stems are grotesquely swollen and in this sense resemble those of a miniature baobab. In time these short stems become covered with lichen, giving them extra character. Small, rounded, succulent leaves occur along the silvery brown stems, with attractive inflorescences of light blue flowers presented at the shoot tips from spring through to late autumn. This species is found in soil-filled cracks and crevices along the edges of sandstone gorges in northern Pondoland. Also occurs on cliff faces.

Plectranthus hadiensis

Hairy spurflower | *Harige spoorsalie*

A plant of variable stature and hairiness that may attain chest height, though most forms typically only reach knee height. The hairy leaves with their toothed margins are medium-sized, and borne on stems that may either trail or remain erect. Plants sometimes bear swollen tubers on the persistent rootstock to enable them to overwinter and survive fires in rocky grassland habitat. Flower colour ranges from mauve to purple, rarely white, with blooms produced during autumn and early winter.

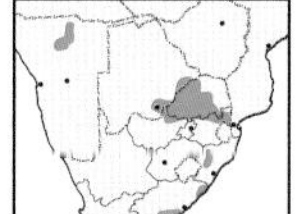

Plectranthus neochilus

Poor man's lavender

Plants grow as a mass of erect to sprawling and creeping stems that carry soft, lightly furry, succulent leaves. The leaves of plants grown in shade are light green and fully expanded, while those of plants grown in full sun are coppery brown and folded lengthwise. In autumn, light blue to purplish-blue flowers are carried in fairly dense, elongated inflorescences. The species has a wide distribution range in eastern and northern South Africa, and beyond into Botswana, Namibia, Zambia and Zimbabwe. It makes an extremely useful ground cover.

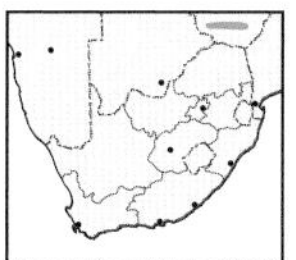

Plectranthus porphyranthus

Plants may attain knee height, but are usually shorter. Their creeping stems are very brittle and bear succulent, hairy leaves that are aromatic and a characteristic blue-grey. The leaf margins are deeply toothed. Bright purple flowers are produced along narrow, ascending inflorescences, at the tips of the stems. They are found on rounded granite koppies growing in full sun. Plants of this *Plectranthus* species were first discovered in the vicinity of Great Zimbabwe.

Plectranthus saccatus subsp. *pondoensis*

Pondo stoep jacaranda

Plants with long stems that trail for up to 5 m. The thick, succulent leaves are smaller than those of the typical subspecies, and are a light green-yellow. Flowering peaks during autumn. While generally resembling the flowers of the more commonly encountered but less succulent stoep jacaranda, the floral tubes are much shorter, with fewer blooms per inflorescence. Occurs along the steep sandstone gorges of Pondoland where it dangles over cliff edges or flexes through the undergrowth of the adjacent forest margin.

Plectranthus tetensis

Bushveld spurflower | *Bosveldspoorsalie*

Stems of this hardy herb trail along the ground. The small, thick leaves have raised veins on the underside, and are usually folded upwards. Inflorescences of bright purple flowers are produced at the ends of the stems during autumn and winter. Flowers have prominent bracts, interspersed with long white hairs. The brittle stems of this straggly plant root along their length, allowing for constant regeneration. Plants are found in bushveld vegetation from Zululand through to Kenya.

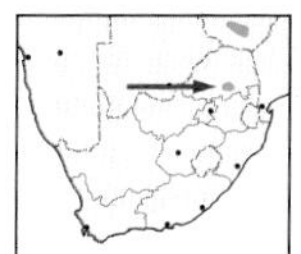

Plectranthus venteri

Sekhukuni spurflower
Sekoekoenie spoorsalie

Quite dense shrubs, multi-stemmed from the base and about thigh high. Each hairy stem is tightly packed with deeply lobed, yellow-green leaves. The flowers are, for a plectranthus, not showy, being quite small and a light violet-purple in colour. Plants of this rather rare spurflower occur mainly in Sekhukhuniland, where they grow among norite boulders in the bushveld. This species is also known from southern Zimbabwe.

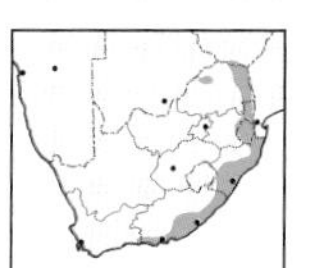

Plectranthus verticillatus

Money plant | *Skindersalie*

This highly variable species has small, succulent, rounded leaves. The form shown here has prominent red markings along the veins on the upper leaf surfaces, and during autumn and winter produces white flowers, lightly speckled with purple. A widespread species, the form figured is from the Lebombo Mountains of Zululand, where it grows in the kloofs and on the forest margins, forming dense mats on the dry rock faces. It makes an ideal subject for a hanging basket.

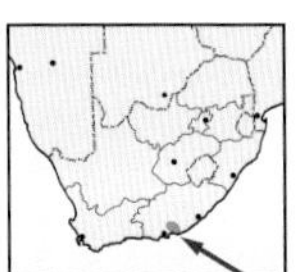

Tetradenia barberae

Fish River iboza

Plants reach thigh height and form dense, well-branched shrubs with succulent leaves, and stems, and swollen, tuberous roots. The small leaves have prominent veins, resembling those of peppermint. The white flowers are borne in late autumn and early winter on upright flower spikes. Unlike *T. brevispicata* and *T. riparia*, plants flower when in full leaf; *T. barberae* is also represented by plants with perfect flowers, i.e. each bloom comprising both male and female functional organs. Plants of this species are known only from the lower Fish River Valley in the Eastern Cape, where they occur in karroid scrub.

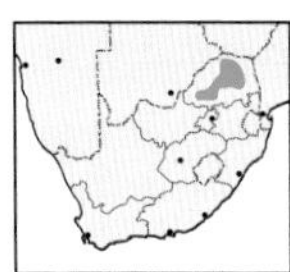

Tetradenia brevispicata

Twiggy, well-branched shrubs, with greyish-black bark on the stems. The leaves are quite small and roundish, with scalloped margins. The leaf undersides are velvety, with veins quite prominent, and the petiole reddish. The sexes are represented by separate plants, with both male and female spikes short and densely set and having tiny, bell-shaped, white to purple flowers. This species occurs in colder regions than the ginger bush. It also flowers in winter, but produces much smaller, less showy blooms that usually appear once many of the leaves have dropped. In warmer sites, the leaves may be largely retained. It is found on dry, rocky wooded hillsides.

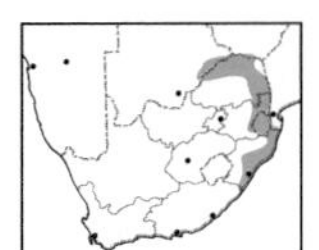

Tetradenia riparia

Ginger bush

This well-known leaf and stem succulent usually attains a height of up to 2 m, forming freely branched shrubs with brittle stems. At times it may appear tree-like. The rounded to oval leaves have a characteristic gingery 'iboza' scent that rubs off readily on contact. During the winter months, when the plants lose their leaves, the well-branched spikes on the stem tips bear profuse white to deep purple flowers. The female and male flowers are produced on separate plants, the male inflorescence generally being larger and more showy. The species is widely distributed throughout the frost-free parts of the summer-rainfall region of South Africa, where it is found in hot river gorges and on rocky wooded hillsides.

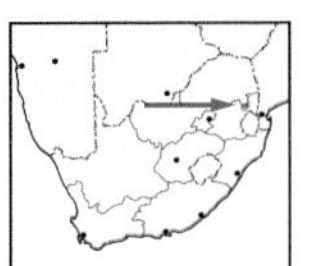

Thorncroftia longiflora

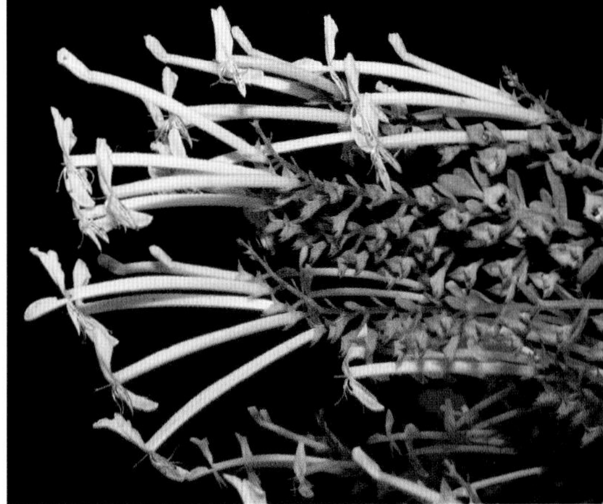

Shrubs grow to knee height, with several upright stems emerging from the base. The small, succulent, blue-grey leaves are clustered on short branches produced along the stem lengths. During autumn, spectacular inflorescences are produced at the purplish stem tips. Each long, tubular flower is presented horizontally and is a bright mauve-pink, the flared mouth purple-flecked on the lobes. It is known only from the vicinity of Barberton, where it grows in pockets of humus overlying rock slabs.

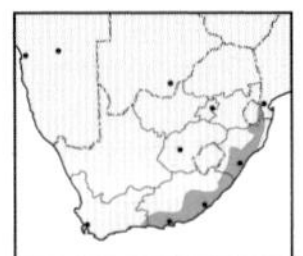

Aptenia cordifolia

Strawberry mesemb | *Aarbeivygie*

Soil-hugging creepers that form tangled, dense mats of thin, angled stems. Heart-shaped leaves are borne in opposite pairs along the length of the stems. Leaf colour varies from light to dark green. In summer, and sometimes even at other times of the year, small, cherry-red flowers are dotted all over the clumps of leafy stems. The species occurs widely through the eastern coastal parts of South Africa, but has also become naturalised in other parts of the country. Plants are useful for binding soil, even on steep embankments, and are often cultivated for this purpose.

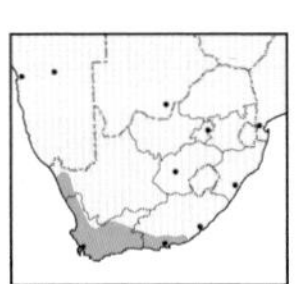

Carpobrotus edulis subsp. *edulis*

Sour fig | *Suurvy*

Plants of this hardy species form dense mats, given their extensive and robust trailing stems. The leaves, which are held upright, are green, tinged with purple along their margins and may be straight or slightly curved. In cross-section the succulent leaves are triangular. Large, yellow flowers (7–9 cm in diameter) with many radiating petals are produced throughout the summer months; these blooms turn pink on fading. The fleshy fruits are both fragrant and edible. Plants are found in exposed, sunny locations.

Delosperma gratiae

These low-growing plants have well-branched, purple stems, with pairs of narrow, succulent and glistening leaves along their lengths. The leaves are slightly grooved on their upper surfaces. The flowers have dark maroon sepals, with blushing pink petals, fading slightly towards their tips. Plants flower during summer and autumn. Like many other members of the genus, this species may be found growing in shallow rock pockets and cascading down protected rock faces in semi-shade.

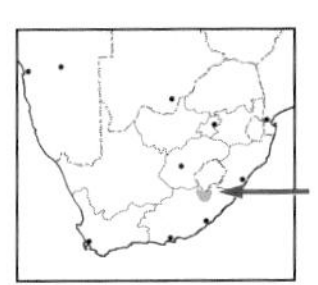

Delosperma scabripes

Plants with trailing stems of over 1.5 m. While the narrow leaves and shoot tips are highly succulent, the older stem sections are much less so, and turn a straw colour; these older sections also tend to become leafless with age. The narrow diameter of the stems, at less than 1 mm, and the profusion of the purple blooms throughout much of the year make this species suitable as a subject for hanging baskets or large container pots. In bright sunlight the leaves turn a rich maroon-purple. Plants are found in full sun to semi-exposed positions on rock ledges, from where their trailing stems cascade down the rock faces. This species can also be used to partly screen, and so relieve, the starkness of retaining wall blocks.

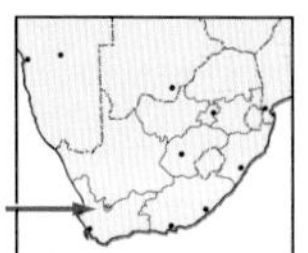

Didymaotus lapidiformis

A miniature, soil-hugging leaf succulent with fat, angled leaves. Leaf shape and colour closely resemble the pebbles among which it grows. Single flowers, often two per plant, are light to bright pink with white towards their centres. These are carried in spring. This remarkable plant is threatened in its very arid natural habitat in the Ceres Karoo, and specimens should never be collected from the wild.

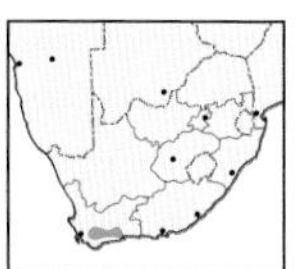

Drosanthemum speciosum

In its natural habitat the species grows as little more than a scraggly shrublet consisting of a few thin branches only. In cultivation, plants develop into large, ball-shaped shrubs. Leaves are small, elongated like jelly beans, and a bright, light green. In their arid natural habitat plants usually bear very few flowers. However, in cultivation, under more amenable growing conditions, the cannon-ball-sized plants are profusely covered in crimson-red flowers during spring. The species is indigenous to the Worcester-Robertson Karoo, eastern Little Karoo, and the southwestern parts of the Western Cape.

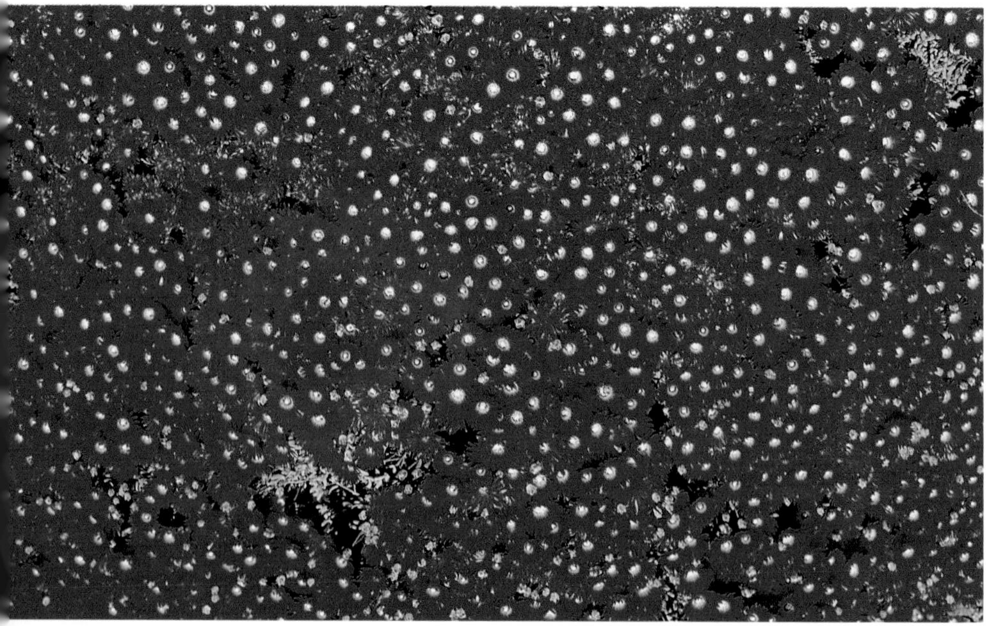

Frithia pulchra

Fairy elephant's foot
Olifantsvoet

Tiny, flattened rosettes, usually with only the tips of the leaves exposed above ground level. In the dry season, the plants disappear entirely and often only a cluster of small, empty tubes in the soil indicate the presence of the species. The leaf tips have a round outline. In shape and texture, they resemble tiny elephants' feet. Flowers appear in spring, are bright pink and quite large for such a small plant. Plants usually grow on shallow rock pans in a thin layer of soil, among pebbles that resemble the shape of the leaf tips. The species occurs on the Magaliesberg only.

Khadia acutipetala

Khadiwortel

Low-growing plants that form small mats. The blue-green to dark green leaves are three-angled towards their tips, becoming near-cylindrical towards their base. Each leaf may attain a length of over 3 cm. Plants possess a thickly branched taproot. During mid-summer, pink to magenta flowers are produced that open during periods of bright sunlight. They occur in soil pockets between rocks, where they are exposed to full sun, mainly around Gauteng. The taproot has traditionally been harvested to produce *khadi*, a strongly narcotic brew.

Khadia alticola

By virtue of their tightly packed leaf bases, these plants form small, matted mounds between the rocks among which they are found. The three-angled leaves are dark green and just over 1 cm long. During mid-summer the uniformly pink flowers open when exposed to sunlight. This is a high-altitude species, found only above 2 000 m in shallow, sandy pockets above a quartzitic substrate. Plants are most likely to be encountered in the Steenkampsberg. Here they receive high rainfall and substantial mist.

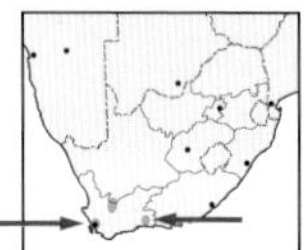

Lampranthus glaucoides

Multi-branched, ankle- to knee-high shrubs with thin, purplish, wiry branches. They carry small, angled, jelly-bean-shaped leaves. These leaves vary from a dull, dusty green to a bright, light green. A profusion of single flowers is carried in spring, turning the plants into golden yellow balls. The species occurs in the Western Cape.

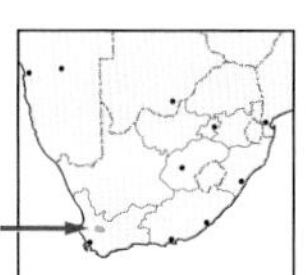

Lithops comptonii

Plants are two-leaved and grow with their flattened, kidney-shaped surfaces flush with the ground. Leaf colour, a greyish, army-green, is very similar to that of the surrounding pebbles. In the dry summer months the remains of the leaves above ground shrivel. Flowers appear in spring and are quite large and yellow, with white centres. The species is more or less restricted to the Tanqua Karoo, a very arid region.

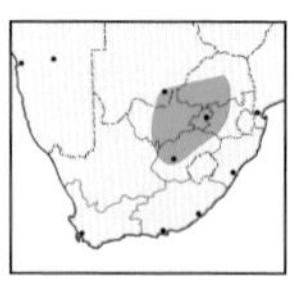

Lithops lesliei subsp. *lesliei*

Stone faces
Beesklou

These miniature succulents grow flush with the ground. Only the flattened surfaces of the two leaves are visible between the pebbles among which they grow. Each leaf is broadly kidney-shaped and the surface is light brown and mottled with irregular, greenish striations, often blending with the surroundings. Flowers eventually emerge from the small, central cavity created by the arrangement of the leaves. They are bright yellow and quite large for such a small plant, often entirely hiding the leaves. The subspecies is widely distributed in central southern Africa.

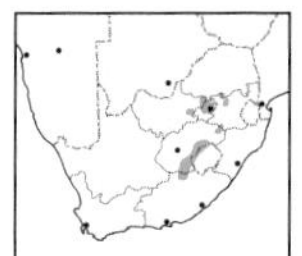

Mossia intervallaris

Plants grow as a network of thin, wiry stems that form a dense, grass-like 'lawn' in their preferred habitats. The stems are reddish-pink and support angled, stubby light green leaves that are fat with accumulated water. Flowers have numerous thin, flat petals that shimmer a brilliant white in the moonlight. Flowering takes place in spring. This is one of only a handful of night-flowering *vygies*. Most members of this family open their colourful flowers during the middle of the day. They occur in shallow rock pans that are covered in thin soils. The species is found in a few scattered colonies in central South Africa, typically in grassland vegetation.

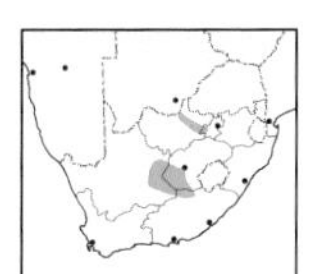

Nananthus vittatus

Brakveldvygie

Plants grow as small, multi-headed clusters that in time become low, dome-shaped mounds. Leaves are soft, rather brittle and keeled on the lower surfaces. They are dark green and have numerous, tiny black dots on both surfaces. Flowers appear in spring. They are bright yellow and the petals have darker brown, central lines. These aloe look-alikes are typical grassland or savanna species in central South Africa.

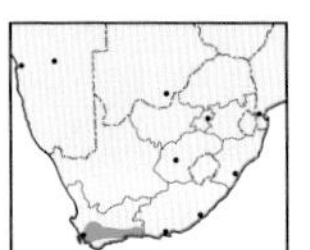

Oscularia deltoides

Plants are erect to sprawling, low-growing shrublets that carry very small leaves on thin, wiry stems. The leaves are blue-green, deltoid to triangular in shape. The margins carry short, stubby protuberances resembling teeth. Flowers are dull pink. The species occurs in a broad band across southern South Africa.

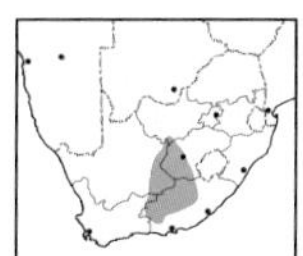

Ruschia intricata

Doringvygie

Plants grow as robust shrubs often over 0.5 m tall. The thin, but sturdy stems and branches carry small, cylindrical, fat leaves. These are dull green in colour. An interesting feature is the very sharp spines – a structure not often associated with vygies – which are carried on the stems. Although quite small, the flowers are bright pink and borne in profusion, often covering the shrubs in spring. Plants are widespread above the severe inland escarpment in central South Africa, particularly in the northern Eastern Cape and southern and central Free State.

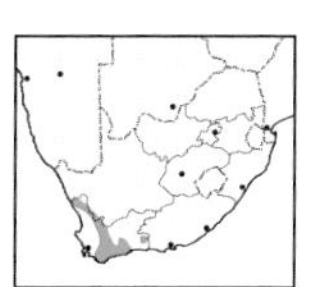

Ruschia lineolata

Rankvygie

This creeper forms a dense, carpet-like network of thin, but strong stems that hug the soil or rocks over which it grows. New stem growth tends to be pinkish, while old stems are greyish-brown. Leaves are short, stubby, angled and quite densely set along the stems. Flowers are pink with longitudinal white lines running along the centres of the petals, and central cone-shaped clusters of whitish pink stamens. Flowers are produced in profusion and virtually cover the plants in spring. Plants grow very well in cultivation and can tolerate very low temperatures of down to –13 °C.

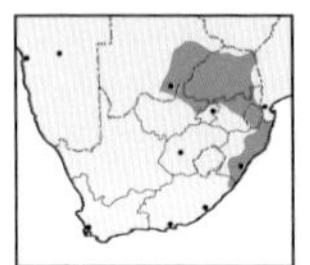

Adenia digitata

Finger-leaved adenia | *Bobbejaangif*

Plants are multi-stemmed scramblers attaining a height of up to 2 m, with shoots arising from a swollen underground stem. The leaves are dark green above, blue-grey below, and almost always five-lobed (palmate), so resembling a hand. These lobes are highly variable in shape, though, with each one either entire or deeply dissected. Additionally, leaf markings vary, with young shoots in particular presenting attractive, silvery markings along the upper veins. The creamy, tubular flowers are produced during spring and early summer, followed by the capsular, red fruit.

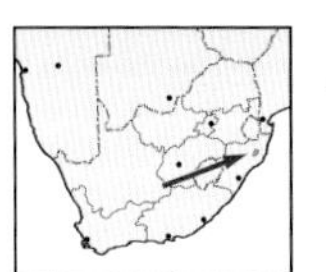

Adenia fruticosa subsp. *trifoliolata*

Zululand greenstem | *Zululand-bobbejaangif*

Plants of this species are tree-like, with greatly swollen aerial stem bases, and prominently swollen roots that are often half exposed above the soil surface. The thickened stems are grey with horizontal green stripes, branching near the base, and giving rise to thin, whip-like shoots that climb, using tendrils, into the vegetation above. The smooth leaves, which are almost round in outline, are deeply three-lobed, lighter below with obvious veins. Male and female flowers are borne on separate plants, fewer female plants typically being encountered in the field. Both flower types are bell-shaped and a greenish-yellow, appearing first in early spring. The spherical fruits are dark green, with distinct lighter mottling when immature, becoming orange-green when fully ripe. This is a bushveld species, restricted to northern Zululand.

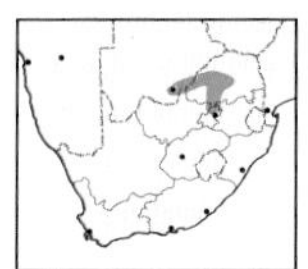

Adenia glauca

Bobbejaangif

The swollen stem base of this adenia is more pronounced than that of *A. fruticosa*, being even more 'bottle-shaped'. From the apex of this blue-grey organ several smooth, trailing shoots extend, bearing five-lobed, greyish leaves. Orange-yellow flowers appear from spring to mid-summer. They occur in clusters along the pendulous stems, male and female flowers being borne on separate plants. Plants may flower before the first new leaves of the season appear. This deciduous species occurs in rocky places in dry bushveld or on sandy soil.

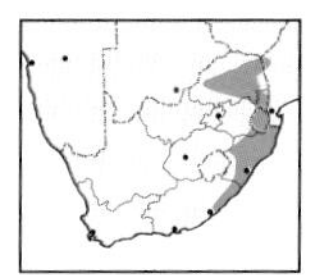

Adenia gummifera

Snake vine | *Slangklimop*

Plants with long, sometimes alarmingly snake-like stems that trail vigorously along the ground and up into the forest canopy. The stems, which may be as thick as one's neck, are blue-grey with white, powdery stripes along their length. The leaves are glaucous, with three nerves arising from the base. They are variously lobed, but often resemble a butterfly in general outline. The insignificant female and male flowers are greenish-cream and produced during early summer. The oval-shaped fruits are leathery and straw-coloured when mature. Plants prefer bushveld and coastal forest habitats.

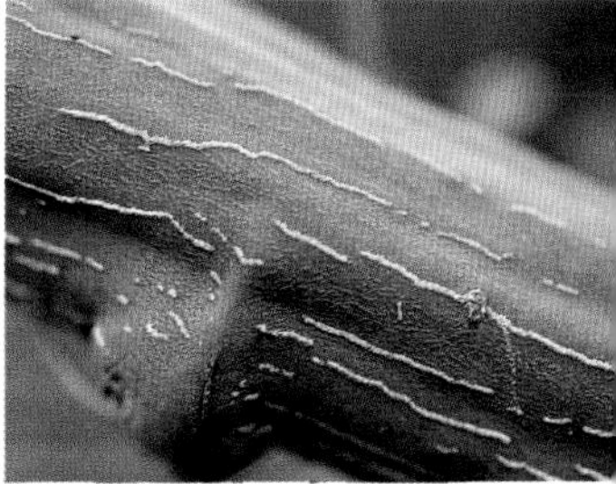

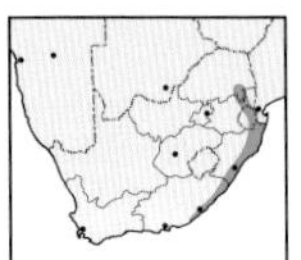

Peperomia blanda

Large wild peperomia

Plants are shin high, with brittle pink or green stems and succulent leaves, each of which is prominently three-veined from the base. Because of their light hairiness the leaves are dusty in appearance compared with other genus representatives in our region, all of which are smooth and shiny. In late summer and autumn, green upright spikes are borne from the stem apex and leaf axil. Each is densely packed with minute flowers. *P. blanda* tolerates considerable drought stress in the dry, rocky, river valleys that it inhabits. Here it grows in soil pockets between boulders or on rock ledges, always in light shade.

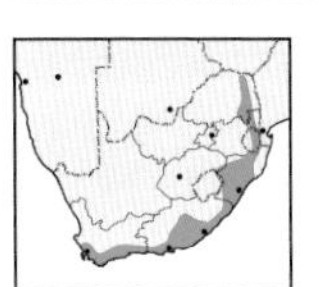

Peperomia retusa

Wild peperomia

Plants form large mats because of the leaning succulent stems that root at the nodes. The egg-shaped leaves are arranged alternately, which distinguishes this species from *P. tetraphylla* (in which the leaves are arranged in whorls of three or four). Leaves are normally hairless and shiny. Minute green flowers are produced throughout the year, widely spaced on short, erect spikes. These inflorescences are produced from both the stem apex as well as further down the stem.

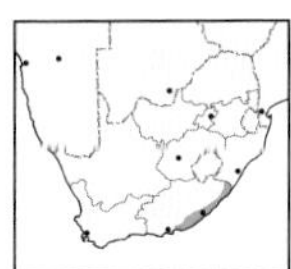

Peperomia rotundifolia

Plants resemble a miniature form of the exotic tickey creeper (*Ficus pumila*) as they work their way over boulders or tree trunks. The thin stems root at the nodes, keeping the plant in close contact with the rock face or branch. Each small leaf is round and more or less parallel with the surface on which it grows. Short, vertical spikes of minute flowers are produced at the shoot ends during autumn and winter. Found in deep shade in moist, coastal forests.

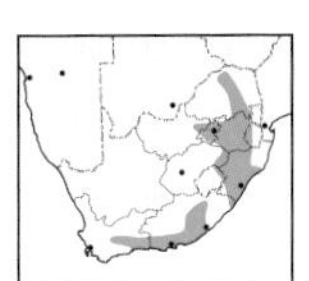

Peperomia tetraphylla

Plants with succulent stems rooting at the lower nodes, so forming an ankle-high mat. The egg-shaped leaves are succulent, smooth and shiny and are usually presented in whorls of four. The lower leaf surface is paler than the upper, which is a dark green with three pale stripes highlighting the main leaf veins running from the base. This feature is not usually as obvious as in *P. blanda*. Erect inflorescences bear tiny flowers towards their tips; such spikes are produced only from the shoot tips rather than from lower down the stem.

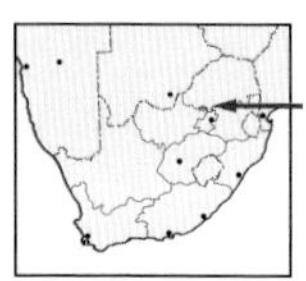

Anacampseros species

Haaskos

This undescribed species has small, shiny, almost globular leaves that are tightly packed on thin stems that hardly reach 5 cm in length. White, thread-like appendages occur between the leaves. The tips of the branches pinch off under environmental stress to yield perfectly round, cottonball-shaped structures that can be blown along the ground by a light breeze, rooting where they settle. Flowers are borne in summer. They are quite large for such a small plant and are a pleasant pink colour. Plants, which occur in rocky grassland, are restricted to a small area in the Magaliesberg Mountains near Pretoria.

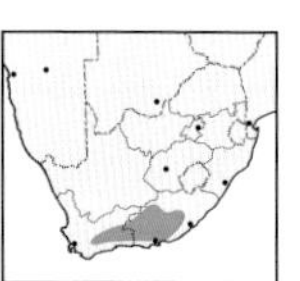

Anacampseros arachnoides

Plants are about 10 cm tall, comprising a cluster of closely packed shoots arising from a succulent, tuberous rootstock. The fleshy leaves are brown-purple and almost as thick as they are wide, with a minute spine at their tip. The leaves are so densely packed as to hide the stem, and when young are covered with a spiderweb-like mat of fine, grey hairs. In mid-summer, white to pinkish flowers are produced on sparsely branched inflorescences presented above the shoots. These short-lived blooms only open when exposed to bright sunlight, the petals curling right back to reveal bright yellow anthers. Plants are usually found in full sun between rocks on dry slopes, or in the partial shade of bushes in the Western Cape and the Great and Little Karoo.

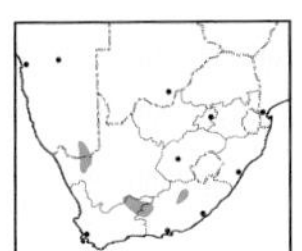

Avonia papyracea

Gansmis

These small herbs scarcely even look like plants. Several cylindrical stems of about 1 cm diameter and up to 10 cm long are produced by, and radiate from, a succulent taproot. These stems bear pure white overlapping scales (stipules, leaf bracts) that completely hide the tiny fleshy leaves below. The creamy white flowers comprise five rounded petals positioned at right angles to what appears to be a central ring of yellow anthers. Plants are highly cryptic and well camouflaged. They resemble the quartzitic pebbles among which they are found in karroid veld.

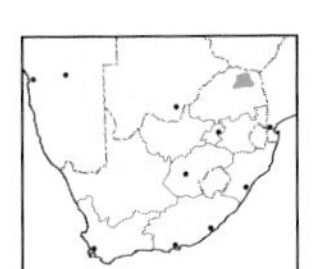

Avonia rhodesica

Moerhoutjie

Plants are miniature herbs that resemble silvery hedgehogs. Each of the several erect stems is only about 3 cm tall. The minute green, fleshy leaves are almost entirely covered by membranous waxy scales (stipules), which are silvery white. Solitary white to pink flowers are produced at the stem apex, but are usually half hidden by the apical stipules. They grow in full sun in what seems to be unbearably hot conditions, with their tuberous roots wedged firmly into cracks on rounded granite koppies, or in small colonies found in very shallow soil pockets overlying these rocky domes. Used traditionally by Zimbabweans as a narcotic additive to beer.

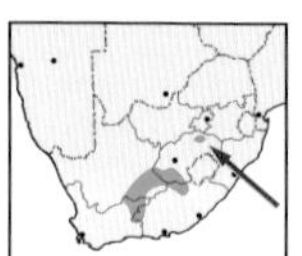

Avonia ustulata

Moerplantjie

Plants reach only thumb height. Succulent tuberous roots support a single stem with thin, finger-like branches of various lengths. These are covered in minute, pinkish leaves that are almost completely hidden by bract-like, silvery scales (stipules). The overall effect is of a plant that resembles a goose dropping. They are well camouflaged in their rocky habitat where they grow in shallow soil pockets overlying rocky outcrops. They may be found either exposed to full sun, or in the light shade of bushes in the Karoo. Used traditionally in beer making, and as a yeast substitute.

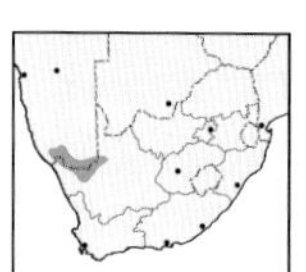

Ceraria namaquensis

Namaqua porkbush | *Wolftoon*

Highly branched shrubs to small trees, reaching a height of up to 3 m. The branches are forked and have dull, silvery grey bark. Tiny, succulent green leaves are arranged in clusters on little shoots on all sides of the stem. These fall off during the dry season, giving the branches a scarred appearance. During mid-summer, numerous small white to purple-pink flowers are borne in clusters near the branch tips. This species is concentrated largely on arid slopes in the lower Orange River system.

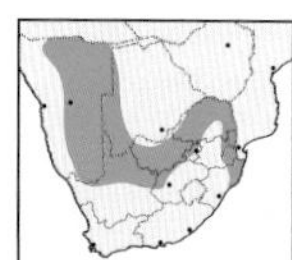

Portulaca kermesina

Vygiebossie

This species of the purslane family presents several mostly erect stems to mid-shin height, each with linear to tapering bluish-green leaves. These are arranged opposite each other, and are quite rounded in cross-section. Long, hair-like leaf bracts are present at the nodes. In summer one to six bright carmine flowers are produced in clusters at the shoot tips. Plants may be found in a variety of hot, dry habitats with sandy soils, from open woodland in the bushveld to old cultivated lands.

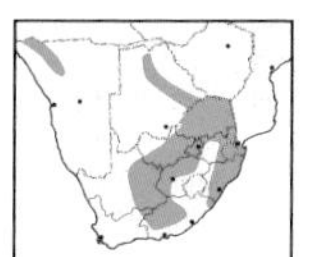

Portulaca quadrifida

Wild purslane

The succulent stems are prostrate, rooting where the nodes contact the soil, and have opposite, succulent, green leaves. Many white, hair-like stipules are evident as tufts between the leaves, and particularly at the stem apices where the yellow flowers are produced during spring and summer. The plants become more reddish when stressed, and die back under extreme drought to their small, swollen taproots. They form colonies in shallow rock pockets in partial shade, often on rock ledges in the drier river valleys.

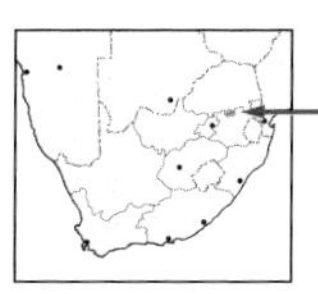

Portulaca rhodesiana

A minuscule succulent annual. The species is considered a pioneer, emerging from seed with the onset of the rains. Each plant grows no taller than about 7 cm and has thin, pinkish-red stems and small, globular leaves the colour of red grapes. The leaf undersides can be lighter, even white below. Tiny, pink, bell-shaped flowers are produced at the ends of the stems during late summer. Plants are restricted largely to Zimbabwe, where they are found growing in full sun in shallow soil pockets overlying granite outcrops. In South Africa, known only from the Witbank region.

Portulacaria afra

Pork bush | *Spekboom*

Plants are robust shrubs to small trees reaching twice the height of an adult. The thick stems and branches are densely covered with succulent, stalkless leaves of a bright green to pale grey. The leaves resemble those of some *Crassula* species, though they are somewhat smaller. When flowering during summer, they make a colourful blaze across the landscape, with their light pink to deep red flowers. They can form dense stands in the Eastern Cape thicket (*spekboomveld*). The pork bush is host to the mistletoe, *Viscum crassulae*.

Talinum caffrum

Porcupine root | *Ystervarkwortel*

Plants are highly variable in size across their distribution range, sometimes reaching mid-shin height. Larger plants are usually prostrate, while smaller ones are erect. Succulent, often trailing stems are produced annually from a thickened, turnip-shaped tuber. The leaves are arranged alternately and their shape varies, although the leaf margins are always rolled under a little. Rich yellow flowers are produced from the leaf axils during summer, each lasting only a day. The fruits are capsules.

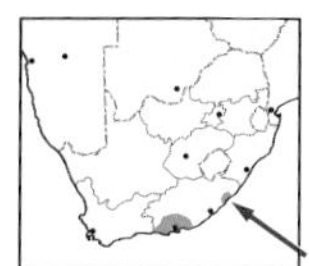

Viscum crassulae

Voëlent

These plants grow as parasites on the pork bush (*Portulacaria afra*) and although their stems vary from darker to more yellowish-green than those of their hosts, they look remarkably like extensions of branches of this succulent shrub or tree. Leaves are yellowish-green, coin-shaped and uncannily resemble those of the host. Flowers are exceedingly tiny and insignificant, but the fruits are a bright orange-red. The species occurs predominantly in the Eastern Cape, but has also been recorded from Durban and Cape Town, where it has possibly been introduced along with cultivated material of *Portulacaria afra*.

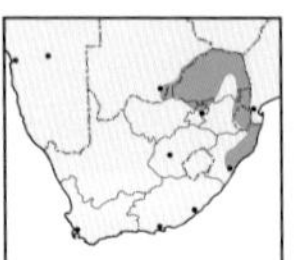

Cissus quadrangularis

Succulent-stemmed wild grape

Plants are robust climbers on trees, forming smothering, curtain-like masses. The succulent, jointed stems are characteristically four-angled, with purple along the winged edges. Most stems are about as broad as a finger, producing leaves between the joints opposite a long tendril. However, plants appear mostly leafless, as these simple organs, found near the stem apices, are dropped soon after being formed. Greenish flowers are produced in branched inflorescences during summer, followed by green warty fruits that turn red on ripening. The preferred habitat is thicket and dry woodland.

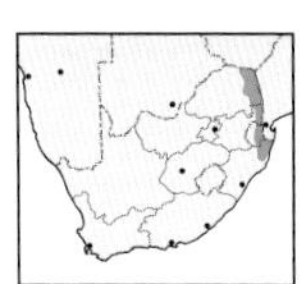

Cissus rotundifolia

Bushveld grape

Using tendrils, plants climb into the surrounding bushveld vegetation, their stems angular and well branched. Very thick, succulent leaves are arranged alternately. The leaf margins, which may sometimes be red, are bluntly toothed. The leaves are characteristically folded upwards along their mid-ribs. Yellow flowers are produced in open, branched inflorescences during early summer, followed by grape-like fruits that are reddish-brown when mature. Often found on rocky outcrops and cliff edges along adjacent forest margins.

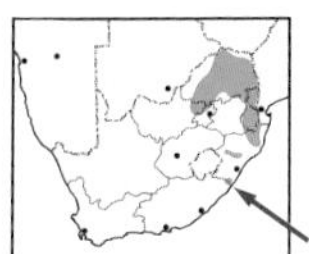

Cyphostemma woodii

Hairy grape bush | *Bobbejaandruif*

Dense shrubs or occasionally climbers that have a swollen stem base (caudex). They may reach thigh height and bear succulent, hand-shaped leaves. These are light green and have a serrate margin. The flowers are yellow and presented in open, branched inflorescences during summer. The berries are green, turning black, and bear spiny, red hairs. The preferred habitat is on hot, exposed rock surfaces, where the caudex wedges between the rocks. It may also be found in open woodland.

GLOSSARY

Anther Part of a stamen that carries the pollen. Usually borne apically on a short stalk (filament) and somewhat enlarged.

Areole Specialised, cushion-like structure from which all cactus growth (stems, spines, flowers) occurs.

Bract Small, leaf-like structure, in the axil of which a single flower or inflorescence branch is carried.

Bulb scale Tightly overlapping and compressed, usually fleshy, leaf base found in a bulb.

Calyx Collective term for the components (sepals) of the usually green, outer whorl of most flowers.

Caudex Stem or trunk, or, in the case of succulents, the massively enlarged root-stem continuation.

Chimaera Plant with tissues of differing genetic make-up, resulting from mutation or grafting.

Cladode Fleshy, usually green, leafless pad of a cactus plant. May be flattened or cylindrical.

Corolla The colourful whorl of lobes (petals) of most flowers.

Corona Whorl of appendages between the petals and stamens. Often forms a ring.

Disc floret Small flower carried on the central, flattened, disc-like part of a daisy inflorescence.

Florets Small flowers, usually carried in dense clusters, for example in the daisy family.

Glochids Small tufts of bristly, stubble-like hairs produced by areoles of cactus species.

Herb A general term used to describe non-woody plants.

Internode Part of a stem or twig between two nodes.

Leaf axil Upper angle between a leaf and the twig or stem that carries it.

Medusoid With many heads or branches radiating to all sides from a central part.

Node Point on a stem or twig from which a leaf (or leaves) arises.

Pachycaul Succulent plant that accumulates moisture and nutrients in the continuum between the root and stem. This part then usually becomes abnormally thickened into various fattened shapes, often bottle-like.

Papilla Soft nipple- or club-shaped protuberance.

Petiole The stalk of a leaf.

Pseudo-flower An inflorescence that resembles a single flower. Also known as a cyathium; typical of *Euphorbia*.

Raceme Type of inflorescence where stalked flowers are borne consecutively along a single axis, with the oldest flowers carried lower-most.

Ray floret Small, colourful flower carried on the margin of the flattened, disc-like part of a daisy inflorescence. Petals of a ray floret are usually fused and appear to be single.

Rhizome Usually horizontal, under-ground stem that produces new growth above-ground each growing season.

Rosulate Arrangement of leaves radiating from a central point, typically the apex of a stem.

Scandent Climbing, scrambling plant that does not have tendrils (thread-like structures that some plants, e.g. vines, produce to cling to support structures).

Sepal One of the outer, usually green, parts of a flower. Collectively the sepals comprise the calyx.

Stamen One of the male reproductive organs of a flower. Usually consists of a stalk (the filament) and the anther (tiny knob-like enlargement at the stalk tip).

Stigma Usually head-shaped part of the female reproductive organ of a flower on which the pollen germinates.

Stipule Scale-like appendage at the base of the leaf stalk of some plants.

Tubercle Tough, usually hardened, white or green protuberance on a plant part, often the stem and/or leaves.

INDEX

Scientific names in *italics*
English common names in **bold**
Afrikaans common names in roman